To Berenice

SP 98/2   11·95

RARY
AN CO
LEY GF
INGH
12

A Theory of

Shopping

WITHDRAWN

N 0084767 4

A Theory of Shopping

Daniel Miller

NEWMAN COLLEGE
BARTLEY GREEN
BIRMINGHAM, 32

CLASS   306.3
BARCODE 00847674
AUTHOR   MIL

Polity Press

Copyright © Daniel Miller 1998

The right of Daniel Miller to be identified as author of this work has been asserted in accordance with the Copyright, Designs and Patents Act 1988.

First published in 1998 by Polity Press in association with Blackwell Publishers Ltd.

Editorial office:
Polity Press
65 Bridge Street
Cambridge CB2 1UR, UK

Marketing and production:
Blackwell Publishers Ltd
108 Cowley Road
Oxford OX4 1JF, UK

All rights reserved. Except for the quotation of short passages for the purposes of criticism and review, no part of this publication may be reproduced, stored in a retrieval system, or transmitted, in any form or by any means, electronic, mechanical, photocopying, recording or otherwise, without the prior permission of the publisher.

Except in the United States of America, this book is sold subject to the condition that it shall not, by way of trade or otherwise, be lent, re-sold, hired out, or otherwise circulated without the publisher's prior consent in any form of binding or cover other than that in which it is published and without a similar condition including this condition being imposed on the subsequent purchaser.

ISBN 0-7456-1945-2
ISBN 0-7456-1946-0 (pbk)

A CIP catalogue record for this book is available from the British Library.

Typeset in 11 on 13 pt Sabon
by Graphicraft Typesetters Ltd., Hong Kong
Printed in Great Britain by TJ International

This book is printed on acid-free paper.

Contents

Acknowledgements   viii
Introduction   1

1 Making Love in Supermarkets   15
2 Shopping as Sacrifice   73
3 Subjects and Objects of Devotion   111

Notes   156
Bibliography   170
Index   176

Acknowledgements

Writing this book has put me in debt to a great many people. Most of them cannot be named since they are my informants and I have tried as far as possible to retain the anonymity which I promised them. The experience of this research was quite different from any previous fieldwork that I have attempted. Working in other countries I always felt extremely welcome and that I could trade on the 'exotic' nature of my own presence, against the time and information I was asking from others. In North London I am much more likely to be regarded as a mere nuisance requesting time from people who inevitably regard themselves as already extremely busy. I am the more grateful therefore to many people who suffered my presence and attention and gave of their time in a manner I cannot feel sure I would have granted if the roles had been reversed.

The fieldwork would have been a great deal more difficult (and also far less enjoyable) without the companionship of Alison Clarke, especially during the period of initial introduction to each household. Alison is proceeding with her own studies based on this fieldwork, but I can already attest to her abilities as an ethnographer. Her relaxed informality which helped me to deal with the frustrations of fieldwork was also the key to providing access to and in some cases developing friendships with the households we were studying.

This book was not an intended outcome of the ethnography, but developed its own momentum. Quite unlike anything else I have worked on, the manuscript seemed to write itself during the midsummer of 1996. The ideas had been swirling around in my head during and after the fieldwork, but there was one definite catalyst that precipitated crystallization into its present form. This was some conversations with the anthropologist Laura Rival. It was Laura who insisted that I take another look at Bataille, whose work I had previously seen as of little interest, and that I concentrate, in particular, on the way Bataille linked consumption to sacrifice. I am very grateful to her and would note that it was her conversations and inspiration as much as actually reading Bataille that were instrumental in conceiving of this book. I would also acknowledge the value of having the work of DeVault drawn to my attention by Pat Berhu.

Although this essay was conceived outside the larger project, the ethnography upon which it is based was funded as part of my contribution to a research study on Consumption and Identity funded by the Economic and Social Research Council. Finally, several people went out of their way to provide detailed comments on the draft manuscript which have proved very helpful in rewriting this work. These are Colin Campbell, Caroline Humphrey, Laura Rival, Michael Rowlands, Don Slater, Charles Stewart, Nigel Thrift and the anonymous reader for Polity Press, to all of whom I am very grateful. Other useful comments were provided by the postgraduates who form our regular 'drinking' group.

Introduction

This is an essay about shopping. It also an essay about love and devotion within families in North London and it is an essay about the nature of sacrificial ritual. In recent months when people have asked me about the work I am engaged in I have replied that I have written an essay with these three themes. The response has tended to be defensive, often expressing incredulity that an essay could possibly rest secure on the foundations of such an odd trilogy. In return I have been tempted to say that if only they could read the essay they would see why these three topics create a structure with integrity but that I can't hope to be at all convincing while standing chatting with them at a street corner. Here at the start of the essay we – the author and reader – have to begin with the brevity of the street corner. Although my overall case is made in the essay as a whole, an initial argument may be made in a small compass.

I hope to persuade you to read this work from a position of empathy, rather than defensive scepticism, through asking for a little introspection on your part. This is not an essay about what people say about shopping, nor about the journalism, conversations at parties or jibes and condescending remarks people constantly make about this topic. It is not about your longing for that coveted object or about holiday browsing. It is about the activity you undertake nearly every day in order to obtain goods for those people for whom you are responsible – the goods you and they eat, wear and employ in a multitude of tasks. So reflect for a few moments on the shopping you have undertaken in the last week. Routine shopping that is the subject of this essay is rarely exciting and usually soon forgotten. It is largely unreflective. But what does it look like? Although this is of course a hugely diverse activity, what are the typical acts of shopping whose observation led me to create this tripartite edifice?

For present purposes I am hoping you have some experiences in common with people in North London – a strong possibility given the diversity of North London people. You are, however, more likely to be an academic or a student. Perhaps you are a junior male lecturer and last week you went shopping for clothes. You went to three shops: two chain stores (C&A and Marks & Spencer) and a small independent, more fashionable outlet. Your girlfriend was complaining about your wearing things she felt you shouldn't be seen dead in. The relationship between the two of you was not such that you were going to admit how attached you had become to the admittedly now well-worn jeans you had on at the time. You are not in the habit of changing during the day, and you tend to meet up after work, so whatever you buy has to do for work also. At work there are two colleagues on the staff who are better at withering sarcasm than writing papers and don't share the same taste as your girlfriend. You can see a couple of pairs in the independent shop that she might approve, but you can just imagine the response at work. But then anyway would she actually like them – she might hate them. Maybe you should go with her, but then she isn't going to give a toss for your workmates' opinions. OK, it shouldn't really matter very much, and yet it was this that made you spend over an hour between the three shops. And anyway what about yourself – your own taste – shouldn't you have some say? There was a pair you liked, but to be honest it was just the same as those you were out shopping in order to replace. You got really fed up: why are you wasting time when you could be on line looking at that new website? But you really do care about her, and you know this is just the kind of gesture that could make the difference, show her you really are willing to compromise, to make some commitment to the future sharing of taste. In the end you find a pair in C&A that is a more sober (and frankly a whole lot cheaper) version of the independent shop's pair, and just hope she won't notice the label.

Or maybe you are a single mother living on a student grant, who was in a supermarket looking at babybath products. You had a choice of a well-known brand and the supermarket's own brand. The latter was a good deal cheaper and you are in more debt than you care to admit to yourself. But nothing is more important than that child, the mere thought of her sends waves of emotion through you. But then who is to say the brand name is better? Someone once told you it's simply more expensive because they spend money on advertising, and the money saved will help towards the baby carrier you really need, the one that lets you carry her on your front, which would be so much better than having her behind where you can't see her gazing up at you. In the back of your head is a darker thought: a resentment that starts from knowing what else this money could be spent on, like so much else that your daughter has in some sense taken from you. There is that totally unwarranted but much desired expensive pair of shoes that your sister the lawyer was wearing and that hovers guiltily somewhere in your head, but remains well suppressed by your sense of love.

I am suggesting these could be you, or at least you could imagine being them. They are not especially profound thoughts, they may cast you as stereotypes, but I for one will admit that my own shopping thoughts are not very profound and tend to the conventional. Thankfully they are backed up by a mass of routine shopping that simply repeats previous experience so these concerns only come to the surface in a few instances. In both these cases your shopping is dominated by your imagination of others, of what they desire of you and their response to you; it is about relationship to those who require something of you. Often these are relationships of devotion, mainly routine devotion, that may be deep or may be superficial, and are mainly taken for granted, except where the choice becomes a sign that you have shown some concern.

In this essay, as in most of the studies that take place within that sub-discipline called material culture studies, shopping is not just approached as a thing in itself. It is found to be a means to uncover, through the close observation of people's practices, something about their relationships. Indeed it is premised on the idea that this may be a better way of uncovering what is called the lived experience of these relationships than a study that was officially supposed to be about relationships. In other words I could have tried to study these things by more direct enquiry, such as asking the man about his girlfriend or the mother about her daughter. I do not assume that the replies received would lead to the same conclusion as that which emerges from the observation of the purchases that relate to them. Shopping may be a vicarious entry into social relations but, I submit, it may lead much further towards understanding contemporary social relations and their nuances than might have been expected.

In another age or another place, a family is preparing to make a sacrifice to a god, not some special grand sacrifice, just one of the routine sacrifices that mark the new moon. The father has charged his son to select the best of the fruit that has recently come to ripen, that without any blemish. The son collects some, the gods demand it, and without their favours the tree may not produce so well next year. He knows that before they consume these fruits of their labour they should demonstrate their care for the gods who care for them. But the best peaches are so tempting that he simply can't but eat one or two which he manages to convince himself have some token blemish that makes them ineligible. Actually he is quite looking forward to the sacrifice. He is proud of what they have grown that year, he knows full well that his two best friends' families have been less fortunate, and he believes that he has played a key role, since he is convinced that he paid more attention to getting the sacrifices right and that he has said his prayers with that much more devotion. He senses the god's gaze on him, as he grows into a devotee. It is his efforts to please that particular god that helped bless the whole family, and he is not going to let them down. So there is real happiness when he finds a peach that seems entirely perfect and that can be placed at the apex of the sacrificial pile. He also is well aware that at the end of the sacrifice he will present the peach to the priest, and that a well-fed priest is much less inclined to beat him when he gets his prayers wrong.

In this essay a projection onto people undertaking sacrificial rituals such as this one will be used to deepen that understanding which we might gain through mere introspection about what is going on when we go shopping. I have suggested such introspection should not be hard; it should be easy enough to relate to the kinds of shopping discussed here. I suspect also that we are highly resistant to such introspection, that we almost all wish to reject such images of our own shopping activity in favour of a model of shopping as hedonistic materialism that we enjoy abusing. A vicarious journey through sacrifice may therefore be needed to convince ourselves that this is not actually what much of our shopping is about.

Summary of the Argument

The essay is divided into three parts. The first part is a descriptive account of four aspects of shopping derived almost entirely from a year's study of shopping on a street in North London. Chapter 1 begins with ethnographic descriptions of shopping. These demonstrate how shoppers develop and imagine those social relationships which they most care about through the medium of selecting goods. After representing a variety of the relationships that may be developed through the medium of shopping, the remainder of the chapter isolates three characteristics of these shopping expeditions. Though not universal they were common to most of the households observed in the ethnography.

The first of these was the concept of 'the treat'. This was the designation given to any special purchase made with respect to a particular individual or group, often including the shopper. It is argued that this category helps define the rest of the shopping as other than the purchasing of treats. The next observation is of the centrality of thrift, that is the strategies by which shoppers attempt to save money while shopping. Evidence is given for the extraordinary range of opportunities which exist for experiencing shopping as saving money and the alacrity with which shoppers make use of these facilities. While these two characteristics are derived mainly from the observation of shopping, the final category is based entirely upon what people say about shopping in general. This will be termed the discourse of shopping in that it generalizes the normative statements that are made about shopping in the abstract.

The second chapter of this essay starts by completely ignoring the first, in that it makes no mention of shopping. Instead it turns to what at first may appear an unrelated topic: it reviews the various theories which anthropologists have brought to bear on the ritual of sacrifice. The rites discussed include a wide range of ancient and contemporary practices, including those of Africa, the Middle East, Greece and Hawaii which have inspired some of the more important studies. The approach taken here follows the classic study of sacrifice by Hubert and Mauss (1964) in insisting that the ritual of sacrifice is best treated as divided into a number of stages, but that for any of these stages to be properly understood, the ritual must be considered as a whole.

This section will end with a consideration of the French philosopher Georges Bataille's analysis of sacrifice as the key precedent for the current essay in as much as Bataille first suggested that sacrifice and consumption were closely connected and that both could only be understood through a general theory of expenditure. Although I come to disagree fundamentally with Bataille's premises and conclusions, the reasons why I believe him to be wrong play a central role in my argument.

The second half of chapter 2 represents the crux of the essay as a whole. All the previous elements of shopping and sacrifice that have been drawn out in the essay up to that point, are there brought to bear as pieces in a jigsaw which must now be used to create a clear picture. The theory of shopping as sacrifice is presented through a division of both shopping and sacrifice into three stages. The first stage comprises a vision of excess which is found primarily in the discourse rather than in the practice of shopping and has many parallels with writings about violence and the constitutive role of violent expenditure in recent discussions of sacrifice. It is argued that both the discourse of shopping and that of sacrifice represent a fantasy of extreme expenditure and consumption as dissipation.

The second stage consists of the central rites of shopping and sacrifice, whose importance lies in their ability to negate these same discourses. The ritual is thereby turned instead towards the constitution of, and obeisance before, an image of transcendence. The core to this ritual is a splitting of the objects of sacrifice between that which is given to the deity and that which is retained for human consumption. An equivalent central ritual to shopping expeditions is found to be that which transforms a vision of spending into an experience of apparent saving. Subsequently there is a similar split in the forms of transcendence evoked during shopping. That which is implicated in a general sense of thrift becomes the second stage, while that which is directed to an expression of love and other relationships becomes the third stage.

During the third stage the emphasis moves to the dissemination of that which has been sanctified through its having passed through the rites of sacrifice, but which now returns to the sphere of the profane. The recent work of Detienne and Vernant on the importance of eating the sacrifice in such a manner as to affirm the primary social categories of society is placed against a literature on feeding the family by DeVault and other feminist writers on the domestic world in consumer societies. While the second stage was directed towards a general transcendent goal of life established through thrift, in this final stage the social orders of this world are re-established.

The third chapter is concerned to elucidate the consequences of having created this juxtaposition between shopping and sacrifice. It starts by considering the possible levels of the analogy that has been drawn, ranging from mere metaphor to much stronger statements of association or continuity between the two spheres. It then starts to build bridges between the two distinct practices through an examination of changing subjects and objects of devotion. This begins with a consideration of love itself and its relation to sacrificial traditions. It is argued that under the pressure of secularization the romantic ideal of love comes to substitute for religious devotion. Today, under the pressure of feminism, there is growing evidence that romantic love is being in turn replaced by a cult of the infant. The implication is that there remains a sacrificial 'habitus'[1] that transcends the particular subjects of devotion. These findings are compared with other recent writings on love in the sociology of Beck and Beck-Gernsheim and of Giddens.

The focus then turns to objects of devotion starting with the concept of 'inalienable possessions' as developed by the anthropologist Annette Weiner. This is used to demonstrate the potential of material culture within devotional rites. It also leads to a discussion of a duality in modern feminism, between the radical deconstruction of gender and the attempt to uncover and learn from the role played by women in specific cultural contexts. The next object of concern is the house and its relationship to thrift. A summary is provided of anthropological theories that have attempted to explain thrift in peasant, tribal and bourgeois societies respectively. This then is turned back to the problem of thrift as encountered in shopping.

Having examined the development of various subjects and objects of devotion, the final section returns to commodities as the material culture of love. Evidence is presented to suggest that alienable goods in our society have come to occupy a niche comparable to inalienable goods in other societies. This returns to the argument that commodities are used to constitute the complexity of contemporary social relations. In the conclusion a final parallel is drawn between shopping and sacrifice in that both are found to be practices whose primary goal is the creation of a desiring subject. The presence of gods is made manifest by the sense that they desire or demand sacrifice. The shopper is not merely buying goods for others, but hoping to influence these others into becoming the kind of people who would be the appropriate recipients for that which is being bought.

My hope is that much of this ethnography will 'ring true' for you as a reader. Where it does not, I hope I have provided sufficient evidence that it was at least the case for many of the shoppers studied in this ethnography. This essay is called 'A Theory of Shopping', but it does not purport to be either the only possible theory of that phenomenon, nor to account for all the varieties of shopping to be found in all regions. It is primarily a theory of the bulk of shopping, which might be termed routine provisioning, as it was carried out, mainly by housewives, on a street in North London. The theory claims that this shopping can be understood as a devotional rite. There are many other aspects of shopping that are not dealt with here. Equally, the theory suggests that there is an important component of gender that is foundational to this ritual practice, and that most female shoppers become identified with this sense of gender when they carry out mundane shopping. The theory does not, however, attempt to address many other perspectives from which gender may be understood, nor the plurality of practices which pertain to other aspects of these same shoppers' identities. The argument is presented as a series of generalizations, while endnotes are used to present qualifications and additional support from other studies and to situate the findings in terms of some current issues in the literature.

The Setting

For a one-year period 1994–5 I attempted to conduct an ethnography of shopping on and around a street in North London. This was carried out in association with Alison Clarke.[2] I say 'attempted' because, given the absence of community and the intensely private nature of London households, this could not be an ethnography in the conventional sense. Nevertheless through conversation, being present in the home and accompanying householders during their shopping, I tried to reach an understanding of the nature of shopping through greater or lesser exposure to seventy-six households.[3]

My part of the ethnography concentrated upon shopping itself. Alison Clarke has since been working with the same households, but focusing upon other forms of provisioning such as the use of catalogues (see Clarke 1997), car-boot sales and gifts, which follows on from her previous studies of Tupperware (Clarke forthcoming). We generally first met these households together, but most of the material that is used within this particular essay derived from my own subsequent fieldwork. Following the completion of this essay, and a study of some related shopping centres (Miller et al. in press), we hope to write a more general ethnography of provisioning. This will also examine other issues, such as the nature of community and the implications for retail and for the wider political economy. None of this, however, forms part of the present essay which is primarily concerned with establishing the cosmological foundations of shopping.

To date, the study is based on seventy-six households of which fifty-two are in what will be called here Jay Road. Jay Road consists of council (state) housing[4] on one side and a variety of housing types, ranging from small purpose-built maisonettes to large family houses on the other.[5] In order to include a fuller selection of middle-class households in our fieldwork we expanded to households on streets that were almost all adjacent to Jay Road. For the sake of simplicity I have, however, amalgamated these in the account, which will therefore refer solely to 'the street'.[6]

To state that a household has been included within the study is to gloss over a wide diversity of degrees of involvement. The minimum requirement is simply that a householder has agreed to be interviewed about their shopping, which would include the local shopping parade, shopping centres and supermarkets. At the other extreme are families that we have come to know well during the course of the year. Interaction would include formal interviews, and a less formal presence within their homes, usually with a cup of tea. It also meant accompanying them on one or several 'events', which might comprise shopping trips or participation in activities associated with the area of Clarke's study such as the meeting of a group supplying products for the home.

For most of those primarily responsible for household shopping the foundation stone for provisioning is shopping in supermarkets. Britain follows the Continental rather than the North American trajectory of retail development in that the emphasis, until recently, has been on large-scale supermarket and hyper-market development rather than shopping malls, though both areas have seen the growth of planned shopping centres (Reynolds 1993). Since this study was carried out in London, the relevant supermarkets include large isolated shops on highways (though not usually as large as the massive out-of-town hypermarkets), but also smaller high-street supermarkets. The other main sites for shopping are the major high-street chain stores and then more specialist stores for occasional purchases such as electronics and furnishing. There is also a parade of small shops on Jay Road itself. While many of the examples given below are from grocery shopping, the study included a full range of clothes, furnishing and domestic shopping. It did not include the purchase of homes, cars or holidays, nor the consumption of state services.[7] This theory of shopping is thereby biased towards the constant 'provisioning' that provides the dominant activity observed in the ethnography.

▓ ▒ Some Starting Points ▒ ▓

In analysing and writing up the experience of an ethnography of shopping in North London I am led in two opposed directions. The tradition of anthropological relativism leads to an emphasis upon difference, and there are many ways in which shopping can help us elucidate differences. For example, there are differences in the experience of shopping based on gender, age, ethnicity and class. There are also differences based on the various genres of shopping experience, from a mall to a corner shop, and in Clarke's work from gifting to Ann Summers parties.[8] By contrast, there is the tradition of anthropological generalization about 'peoples' and comparative theory. This leads to the question as to whether there are any fundamental aspects of shopping which suggest a robust normativity that comes through the research and is not entirely dissipated by relativism. In this essay I want to emphasize the latter approach and argue that if not all, then most acts of shopping on this street exhibit a normative form which needs to be addressed. In the later discussion of the discourse of shopping I will defend the possibility that such a heterogenous group of households could be fairly represented by a series of homogenous cultural practices.

The theory that I will propose is certainly at odds with most of the literature on this topic. My premiss, unlike that of most studies of consumption, whether they arise from economists, business studies or cultural studies,[9] is that for most households in this street the act of shopping was hardly ever directed towards the person who was doing the shopping. Shopping is not therefore best understood as an individualistic or individualizing act related to the subjectivity of the shopper. Rather the act of buying goods is mainly directed at two forms of 'otherness'. The first of these expresses a relationship between the shopper and a particular other individual such as a child or partner, either present in the household, desired or imagined. The second of these is a relationship to a more general goal which transcends any immediate utility and is best understood as cosmological in that it takes the form of neither subject nor object but of the values to which people wish to dedicate themselves.

It never occurred to me at any stage while carrying out the ethnography that I should consider the topic of sacrifice as relevant to this research. In no sense then could the ethnography be regarded as a testing of the ideas presented here. I had already carried out ethnographic research on shopping in Trinidad (Miller 1997: 243–301), which proved to have as many differences from as similarities with that encountered in North London. The literature that seemed most relevant in the initial analysis of the London material was that on thrift discussed in chapter 3. The crucial element in opening up the potential of sacrifice for understanding shopping came through reading Bataille.[10] Bataille, however, was merely the catalyst, since I will argue that it is the classic works on sacrifice and, in particular, the foundation to its modern study by Hubert and Mauss (1964) that has become the primary grounds for my interpretation. It is important, however, when reading the following account to note that when I use the word 'sacrifice', I only rarely refer to the colloquial sense of the term as used in the concept of the 'self-sacrificial' housewife.

Mostly the allusion is to this literature on ancient sacrifice and the detailed analysis of the complex ritual sequence involved in traditional sacrifice. The metaphorical use of the term may have its place within the subsequent discussion but this is secondary to an argument at the level of structure.

1
Making Love in Supermarkets

For many purposes the main division in the street where I conducted fieldwork lies between the council estates on one side and the private housing on the other. But the significance of this division cannot always be assumed. Although she lives in an owner-occupied maisonette, Mrs Wynn comes across immediately as quintessentially working class. Her husband is an electrician but has been unemployed for several months owing to an injury. She is a childminder, taking into her home other people's children while they are out working. Between his injury and the fact that someone recently ran into their car while it was parked outside their house, they were not having an easy time of it. Nevertheless, as often proved to be the case, her concerns in shopping bear little upon the contingencies of the moment, and relate more to longer-term issues surrounding the personal development of each member of the family. She was pretty fed up with the consequences of these unexpected events, but shopping as a topic drew her back to things that at one level were more mundane. But these were relationships which she cared about a great deal and was constantly thinking about and forming strategies to deal with. In conversation she notes:

A[11] My husband is quite fussy vegetable wise and he's a big meat eater, but yes I've been doing a lot of stir fries because I found I could get him to eat a lot more vegetables if I do stir fries, and he likes Chinese. He likes spicy stuff. He's got a lot better than when I first met him because his mum's Irish and over cooked everything and was pretty basic and he's got so much better in the years.

Q Do the kids eat the same as him?

A No. Jack my son's got very fussy, definitely in the last year. I would say he's a good vegetable and fruit eater but he's the basic chips and burger and I'm afraid so.

Q Do you cook separately for them?

A Pasta he loves pasta. Yes, and separate times as well.

Later on in the same conversation she notes:

A I try not to buy a lot of convenience [foods]. I do buy meat that is marinated and stuff like that and then think what can I do with it, but now and again I will sit down and get my books out and have a look. I did it last week just because I was getting a bit tired of things. But also what I will do is buy the sauces and the stir-fry things, stuff like that, and then just add it to everything so it makes a bit of difference, but I seem to get stuck doing the same things over and over again. So, every now and then, I've got to get my books out to remind myself or think of some new things.

Q Is it you that's bored?

A No. He will say as well, we've had this a bit too much. I'm a great chicken eater and he says chicken again!

Later still she starts discussing the purchase of clothing for the family, making it clear that she buys her husband's clothes. She notes that out of preference he would just wear some old T-shirts, and often would then go on to use these as cloths during his work. It's not just his clothing she buys. In practice she prefers not to let him do any of the shopping. She feels that if she lets him shop, then he misses things on the list she has made, or buys himself things like biscuits on a whim.

A So it's more hard work. I'd rather him stay here and look after the children and I'll do it. Then it's a break for me and you know.

These views were reiterated when we were out shopping in a local supermarket. She again noted the problems with getting her children to eat what she wants them to eat rather than what they would choose for themselves. She claimed to be quite strict with the children that she was paid to look after, but with respect to her own children, she tended to be much more lenient – 'anything for a bit of peace and quiet.' Again and again her actual purchases are related back to household preferences. When she buys mint-flavoured lamb at the butcher's she notes in passing that this had gone down really well the week before and that she had been asked to get it again. Equally, some jam tarts purchased previously because they were under offer (going cheap) had been well received. The only exceptions to this orientation to the household in her shopping come with the purchase of some bread rolls and frankfurters for a friend who will be coming round for tea. Also at another point in our expedition she buys a fancy ice cream called Vienetta which she declares is 'a treat for herself'.

By no means all the shoppers I accompanied were like Mrs Wynn, but she is representative of a core of households. She should anyway be quite a familiar figure from many previous feminist studies of the housewife. The feminist perspective on such housewives will be discussed below, but many researchers have acknowledged that which would be clearly evident here. However oppressive the outside observer might find this subsumption of the individual to her husband and children, the housewife herself insists that she merely expresses thereby a series of responsibilities and concerns with which she strongly identifies and of which she is generally proud.

Mrs Wynn acknowledges that she is constantly monitoring, even researching, the desires and preferences of her household. These include both foundational goods which are expected to be constantly present and available in the house, but also transient desires which arise from a preference for at least a subsidiary element of change and innovation. But she would by no means regard herself as merely the passive representative of these desires. Indeed if she merely bought what the other members of her household asked for, shopping would be relatively easy. The problem is that she wishes to influence and change her husband

and children in quite a number of ways. She is constantly concerned that they should eat healthier foods than those they would choose for themselves. By the same token she wants them to wear either better quality or at least more respectable clothes than those they prefer. She sees her role as selecting goods which are intended to be educative, uplifting and in a rather vague sense morally superior. It is precisely their unwillingness to be uplifted by her shopping choices that creates the anxieties and battles of shopping. In vindicating their decisions, such housewives often lay claim to a wider perspective than that of other family members. They see themselves as having the foresight to prevent the embarrassment and disdain that others might feel if they let their families dress as they choose, or determine their own food choices.

Of course, all these efforts could be reduced to her interests. It could be argued that she is buying better clothes because she feels she will be made to suffer the opprobrium of criticism by others if she doesn't. She buys healthier foods because she would have to look after the person who otherwise becomes ill. But for us to try to figure out whether the constant hassle of arguing with her family, in order to persuade them to adopt her preferences, actually pays some kind of long-term dividend is the kind of daft calculation we may safely leave to economists, socio-biologists and their ilk. There is no reason to suppose that Mrs Wynn engages in any such weighing up of cost or benefit. As far as she is concerned, the reasons that she researches their preferences and equally that she then tries to improve upon them are the same. Both are assumed by her to represent the outcome of a responsibility so basic that it does not need to be made explicit or reflected upon. In short, her shopping is primarily an act of love, that in its daily conscientiousness becomes one of the primary means by which relationships of love and care are constituted by practice. That it is to say, shopping does not merely reflect love, but is a major form in which this love is manifested and reproduced. This is what I mean to imply when I say that shopping in supermarkets is commonly an act of making love.

One could use other terms than love. Care, concern, obligation, responsibility and habit play their roles in these relationships. So also may resentment, frustration and even hatred. Can these latter be the ingredients of something we may properly term love? As long as it is clear that we understand by this term 'love' a normative ideology manifested largely as a practice within long-term relationships and not just some romantic vision of an ideal-ized moment of courtship, then the term is entirely appropriate. Love as a practice is quite compatible with feelings of obligation and responsibility. As Parker (1996) has noted, love for infants is inevitably accompanied by hatred and resentment, and this is perhaps rather more evident for partnerships. The term is cer-tainly justified by ethnography in as much as these shoppers would be horrified by the suggestion that they did not love the members of their family or that there was not a bedrock of love as the foundation of their care and concern, though they might well acknowledge some of these other attributes as well.

I never knew Mrs Wynn well enough to be able to gain a sense of the more intimate moments within her household. I don't know how free she felt about expressing her love in explicit forms. In general, a reticence with regard to more overt expres-sions of emotion is regarded as a typically British characteristic, and was commented upon by those born elsewhere. But this reticence about love need not imply its absence, so much as its being essentialized as so natural that it becomes embarrassing to feel the need to express it. One consequence of this reticence is that love has come to be primarily objectified through everyday practices of concern, care and a particular sensitivity to others, within which shopping plays a central role.

During the course of this essay the term 'love', which first appears here as the common term by which relationships are legitimated will become used to represent a value that leads us towards the problems of cosmology and transcendence. These terms are not intended to obfuscate or make complex some simple phenomenon. They merely remind us that within a largely secular society almost all of us still see ourselves as living lives directed to goals and values which remain in some sense higher than the mere dictates of instrumentality. Daily decisions are constantly weighed in terms of moral questions about good and bad action indicated in traits such as sensitivity as against style, or generosity as against jealousy. Though these may not be made explicit, the accounts we use to understand each others' actions depend on the continued existence of cosmology as a realm of transcendent value.

The terms 'cosmology' and 'transcendent' suggest values that are long lasting and opposed to the contingency of everyday life. They are intended to imply that although we focus upon the particular persons, children, partners and friends who occupy our concerns at a given moment of time, the way we relate to them is much influenced by more general beliefs about what social relations should look like and how they should be carried out. At one level then, love is a model of one particular type of identification and attachment. It is one we are socialized into and constantly informed about. This ideal is then triggered by an individual, such as a family member who makes it manifest. A relationship then builds its own specificity and nuance which (sometimes) goes well beyond the transcendent model with which we started. When the term 'love' is used, as here, in a more general sense, actual relationships are found to develop on the basis of much wider norms and expectations which pre-exist and remain after the relationship itself.

The term 'love' then indicates more than a claim to affection made during courtship. It stands for a much wider field of that to which life is seen as properly devoted. In later parts of this essay it will be more closely related back to devotional practices in which the term 'cosmology' is more obviously appropriate since the context is more clearly that of religion. The ethnography suggested that just as devotion is the taken-for-granted backdrop to the carrying out of religious rites in other times and places, so in North London love remains as a powerful taken-for-granted foundation for acts of shopping which will be argued to constitute devotional rites whose purpose is to create desiring subjects.

I would call Mrs Wynn a housewife, even though for the present she is the sole wage-earner of the family, because, for her, house-wifery is her principal *raison d'être*. As feminist research has made clear, a person such as Mrs Wynn is more likely to view her earnings as simply part of her housewifery than as a job equivalent to that which her husband would be engaged in were he fit. As someone who identifies with being a housewife, the requests made by her family for particular foods are not viewed with resentment but are in fact desired by her. This is made quite explicit in another conversation with a working-class Cypriot woman.

Q Do you enjoy cooking?
A Yes I do, I'm afraid I do.
Q Does your family appreciate it?
A Oh yes, they do they love the food, my daughter when she comes home she says 'Oh mum food', she opens the fridge as soon as she comes in.
Q Is your husband particular?
A Oh he doesn't like very hot, very spicy food, but no he just eats what he's given really.
Q Does he make any requests?
A Oh I wish he would! No he doesn't.

Here, as is so often the case, there is no evident resentment at being identified unambiguously with housewifery. On the other hand, there is a considerable desire that this should be appreciated by the family members, and not taken for granted. A specific request for an item when shopping is taken as a kind of bringing into consciousness of the role played by the shopper and is most often viewed positively, even if it becomes a cause of contention. The subsequent argument is itself an opportunity for the housewife to demonstrate that she is only contradicting the request because of how much she cares for the person and therefore the consequences of what she buys. In general, the problem many housewives expressed was the lack of valorization, most particularly of the moral, educative and provisioning roles that housewives see as of immense importance. They would not normally use the term 'love' for such concerns, but it is clear from what they do say, that it is love alone that can satisfactorily legitimate their devotion to this work. It is also clear that to be satisfactory the subjects of love should desire and acknowledge that which the housewife sees as her ordinary devotional duty.

In the last two decades we have become far better informed about the work involved in keeping a home going and activities such as shopping. This is almost entirely thanks to a series of important empirical studies of housework inspired by the feminist critique of housewifery as unvalorized labour. Within a short time a normative pattern was uncovered and well documented which suggested that women tended to be largely responsible for the basic provisioning of the household, while men tended to be responsible mainly for extra items that were of particular interest to themselves, but were relatively unimportant in, for example, provisioning for children. Male work outside the home was found to be fully acknowledged through wages and through an endorsement of its centrality to the maintenance of the home as in the phrase 'bringing home the bacon'. By contrast, women's work in the home was not only unpaid but even the homeworker tended to downplay the sheer weight of labour involved in keeping house. This degree of exploitation and the asymmetry of power was reinforced rather than redressed in consumption, where housewives were found to give the best of their labour in meals and comforts to others while often denying themselves the pleasure they strove to create for others.[12]

In general, our fieldwork revealed similar patterns to those uncovered in this previous work, and merely demonstrates that these generalizations still largely hold for the 1990s in this area of North London. Our research thereby also confirms the main conclusion of these other studies as to the basic asymmetry of housework and the exploitation of female labour. By the same token these previous studies provide the bulk evidence for the centrality of love and care as the ideology behind mundane domestic activities such as shopping, to which this case study becomes merely an additional exemplification. The primary examples are these highly conventional expressions of care and concern within households. But there is a wide range of other ways in which love is expressed, which will be illustrated below. Examples include love within egalitarian couples, by the elderly, between friends, siblings and a gamut of other relationships. Even if love is extended to this degree, however, I am obviously not claiming it is ubiquitous. Not every shopping practice is about love; there are others that relate more to selfishness, hedonism, tradition and a range of other factors. What I will claim, however, is that love is not only normative but easily dominant as the context and motivation for the bulk of actual shopping practice.

Some Varieties of Love-making

Sheila, like Mrs Wynn, provides for a nuclear family within a clearly working-class milieu, in this case living in council housing. Her husband Bob works night shifts for the army and she works as a shop assistant. Unlike Mrs Wynn, however, their relationship is based on far more extensive sharing of activities such as shopping. This is in large measure due to the fact that his night shift is more compatible with shopping than her day shift. Beyond this is a more complex relation of gender. He works in the highly macho environment of the army, but is himself a clerk. He constantly expresses preferences for rather macho taste, but it is understood that this covers a rather less forceful disposition and a rather fearful personality. This comes over, for example, in his clear terror of the pigeons that fly around the high street and to which most people give little or no regard. The gender divisions are then traditional but not given, in that they have to be constantly re-expressed to hide what is otherwise a more confident and strong woman. For her part she does indeed want him to shop but because of her sense of love and family devotion she desires at the same time to protect his rather more fragile self-confidence from this aberration from their mutually conservative notions of gender differences.

The result of these contradictions was evident in the constant comic banter between the spouses when I accompanied them both shopping. In turn this was related to a clearly held view as to the importance of easy-going compromise as the foundation to their ideal of how their relationship ought to be. Shopping choices and negotiations then come to play their part in the constant reiteration of what they regard as the positive elements of their relationship. This ideal is made clear in earlier conversations.

A But Sheila is normally easy because she always says to me 'Well we're pretty easy-going.' Like you know as long as we don't hate something, like we'll say Oh alright that's fair enough.

Q What about other opinions?

A No we don't, we're not for things like that. We get what we like. Well to be truthful the kids, they don't. They're like us, really easy-going, 'Oh that's alright yeah, that's it.' Charlotte, when we first did the wallpaper she said 'Oh it's disgusting', but a week later she said 'No it's nice, I like that wallpaper Dad.' Normally the kids are easy-going.

Within this idea of 'easy-going' is negotiated an arrangement whereby the individuality of each family member is made explicit, but the demands that this individuality may put on the group limited. So the father is allowed to have tastes that are seen as natural to a 'proper man' as in:

A They don't eat what I call proper. The whole household to me. I'm the only one who eats proper meat, what I call meat, I don't call them things beefburgers and all that, I'm talking about lamb chops, pork strips, legs of chicken.

Q Butcher's?

A Yeah a butcher's – exactly. I like my meat. I love my meat.

Similarly, the daughter is expected to have the propensities recognized as normal for a sixteen-year-old girl, but only in as far as they can be put together in a feasible shopping package. Demand for further autonomy is referred back to that individual, unless this seems to her mother to be a 'reasonable' request for special consideration.

A Occasionally she'll ask for something, cotton balls or, and food wise she'll ask 'Oh I like them so and so I haven't had them for a while' You know whatever. She likes them chicken bites doesn't she, she'll say 'dinosaurs [a shape of processed chicken] when are you getting some more dinosaurs', so I say 'If you want it just say what you want' 'cos Charlotte's not a real meat eater I mean she gets on me nerves sometimes.

Q Do you still buy most things for her?
A Oh yes, I'll say to her sometimes the day before 'Do you want a chilli tonight or something or would you prefer just something with chips or', but she'll let me know like in advance though.
Q Things she gets for herself?
A That's her hair things.
Q Clothes, music?
A Well we help with the clothes sometimes, but if she just wants to get a T-shirt, something like that, she'll get herself that out of her pocket money. She gets her hair sprays and hair colour whatever. The cleansing lotion we normally get because she can't use soap and water, so she has to have cleansing, so you know we get that for her.

During the shopping expedition the banter between them consists mainly of criticisms spun off as jokes. Sheila, as many North London housewives today, heads first for the National Lottery, while he takes the list for shopping. On her return he says to me in a loud – to be overheard – voice 'you didn't see how much she spent when she went off to buy cigarettes did you! She gave you the slip that time!' Later she interrogates him about a red-wine casserole sauce for chicken that he seemed to have slipped into the shopping basket without her seeing, and then again about some better-quality coat-hangers. She laughingly notes how 'You are going to see a fight now', and that he had better take them back. Yet this is said in a way that is clearly an acknowledgement that she accepts the purchase as a *fait accompli*. He tries but then fails to choose a jam, since he knows the kids don't like ones with pieces of fruit in, but doesn't know enough to be sure what they do like since 'the kids is her department'. Later at the shampoo counter she pretends she finds one for 'no hair' (since he is receding). 'She always gets one over me' he remarks. A key element within this comic banter is her constant criticism of his lack of shopping skills, for example, his forgetting to pack the bread in such a way as to prevent it becoming crushed. Taken in context, however, these criticisms are a mechanism she uses to affirm that as a man, although he may shop, he is not a natural shopper. He is thereby able to receive such 'criticisms' as praise for his natural manliness, something which he recognizes. I can see him light up with pride at each barb levelled against him. All such criticism is gratefully received.

Their individual shopping choices are part and parcel of the same shoring-up of conventionality. Compared to most shoppers, they tend to a much higher proportion of branded as against supermarket own-label goods. Also their food choices are amongst the most overtly 'British' of any of the grocery shopping observed. Apart from the elderly, most shoppers tend to take advantage these days of the highly cosmopolitan possibilities of the supermarket. But this family's shopping basket has mainly items such as mint sauce, chops, shortbread, corned beef, sage and onion stuffing, vinegar, pork belly and chipping potatoes, which together form a portrait of 'Britishness' in the rather 'bulldoggy' sense that he brings from his workplace. It is this that gives meaning to the cheap 'wine-based' casserole sauce being slipped into the basket as his guilty secret – his French bit on the side.

The couple also have to contend with a problem with their son, which time and again becomes a key point of contention for working-class shoppers on low incomes. Almost invariably sons desire the special football stripes (clothing) for their team and these are extremely expensive. In this case, the new Spurs (a football team) stripe would cost £66, which they really can't afford. In fact, they have resorted to borrowing the money from a building society account which contains funds given to their son from his grandparents. Although at one level they know they are stealing from their own son, they reason that it is more important to be able to provide something which has become a key element in a boy's constitution as a member of his peer group. Indeed, this is precisely the kind of 'love that cannot be denied' which can lead to theft by impoverished families, who, as in this case, would see themselves as scrupulously law-abiding by choice. I could never imagine this couple stealing on their own behalf, but they are simply too driven by love for this not to be imaginable as action on behalf of others. This example also makes clear that love should not be isolated as something opposed to wider social concerns. Here love takes the more exquisite form of parental anxiety over how the son will be treated if he does not live up to the expectation of his peers. Similarly, love may incorporate class consciousness, emulation and other factors discussed in research on consumption (see Slater 1997: 33–99 and Warde 1997: 7–42 for recent examples), in as much as these are turned into intra-household needs and anxieties.

Of course, this couple does not possess the eloquence of writers about household relations, such as the playwright Ibsen. Yet there is no reason why Ibsen could not be properly invoked. The family tensions and contradictions evident in their relationships are not just between individuals fulfilling roles, but revolve around the basic attributions of gender and its burdens of expectations in the form of male strength and female sentiment. These are precisely the issues found in Ibsen's fictional accounts of the classic bourgeois family. Shopping here allows for considerable play with performance and facade and the complex empathy and humanity that allows love to be the instrument rather than the victim of such contradictions. My contention is that this couple (as those writers) often reveal ways in which a larger sense of humanity struggles to express itself within a structure whose fundamentally oppressive nature would otherwise overwhelm them. It is hard to imagine a more unlikely figure of philosophy than Sheila, yet it was clear on the several occasions that I also observed her in the shop where she worked, listening and sometimes chatting extensively to fellow workers and customers, how she strives to bring to this, her second marriage, skills and sentiments gathered from her constant exposure to the trials and tribulations of other people's everyday domestic relations.

My next example requires us to cross, not only the road, but also that considerable boundary between the two major class contexts of British society, in order to review an extract from a much longer discussion about furniture shopping. Here are found a comparatively egalitarian couple, where the husband is said to do as much cooking as the wife, but their core shared interest is in art and design. The husband actually teaches design and the wife has a strong interest in the arts. For them the emphasis on the commonality of taste become a particularly significant expression of their existence as a compatible couple in love.

A Well we needed a sofa. We decided we didn't have enough seating in our house. We had a little sofa, then we had a couple of chairs so it was hopeless. So we were looking for a sofa and they're all so expensive and we were going around everywhere thinking 'Oh no', you know and they were all horrible. So we thought let's go to IKEA, they're fairly cheap there and the things seem fairly sturdy enough. We've got book cases and stuff from there before, and we went along, and we saw a sort of sofa bed we thought we'd get so we could have people come over and sleep, stay over, sort of dual purpose and we nearly went to buy one, and we were on our way out, when we went into the bargain basement corner, and there was this sofa, and we didn't immediately say 'yes that's it', we sort of went 'um yeah'. Actually we hadn't thought of leather, but yeah yellow's OK. Then I suddenly thought that would be just right, that'll just do us just fine so I sat on it while Allen went up to the cashier and said 'yes we want that sofa, I want to pay for it now before someone else gets it' 'cos there was only one like £750 and it was like £400 so and we squeezed it into the back of our Golf (car). It could barely fit, took the legs off. We strapped it on, came home and my brother was like 'Hey you've got a new sofa' so it worked out quite well really. Allen's always worried that the cat's going to be scratching it up and stuff.

Q Does the cat scratch?

A Yeah yeah she just sort of walks around and hangs on. There are a few little bits but it's worn quite well. We're quite pleased with it really. I think it looks pretty good. It doesn't obviously look IKEA or anything so. Some of my friends really hate IKEA so you have to choose carefully what you get from there.

As in the case of the football stripes, this conversation demonstrates the interweaving of intra-household love, here expressed as the taken-for-granted sharing of taste, and the firm eye kept on the effect this has on the image of the couple exposed to external criticism.

These three examples express relationships that are already well established. Shopping can also shed light on relationships that are coming into being. There is a less common but equally germane case of shopping as a specific act of courtship – that is part of a series of activities that enable a couple to decide whether they could or should be regarded as what is so eloquently termed 'an item'. We remain within the middle-class milieu of a young divorced woman, who is both a journalist and student at a design college, shopping with her boyfriend. Although he had not yet moved in with her, they had at least broached the topic of buying a house together. At this stage the crucial factor in shopping was my presence. This was an occasion to learn about each other's taste and forge a relationship in terms of shopping compatibility. But there was also the question as to how they appeared as a couple to an outsider. The sheer effort that I felt they were putting into showing me how happy they were together should not be seen as thereby false. It reflected their own question as to whether, when revealed in the reflected gaze of the anthropologist, they would find themselves to be in love.

They have both just bathed and dressed, they are in jeans, but are equally well trained at looking good in blue denim. Almost every shopping choice is exploited as an opportunity to construct an agreement as to whether to go his way, her way or in a way that could be defined in the future as 'their' way. This started from the decision as to whose car to use. During the journey they are exchanging knowledge about the best place to buy items (mainly car-related items). Although both have said that they do not normally enjoy grocery shopping, they are clearly out to have a good time. They have little gestures of fun, for example, she rushes to pick the bag of tea just before he gets there. She then holds it above the trolley and lets go in a kind of 'plop' gesture, as opposed to merely putting it in. They put their arms around each other, they perform little acts of showing off, such as when she pushes and then 'rides' on the trolley for a couple of feet. At one point she picks up a mini fudge to give him as an immediate gift. They also engage in conspicuous compromise: for example, at one point she picks up butter, he a low-fat spread, they then decide to have small tub of each. The shopping is not only about finding common tastes. Compared to most shoppers she spends quite some time simply picking up items she would not normally have considered. She does not buy any of them, but it is clear that the opportunity for changes represented by her new relationship is also a catalyst for her trying to imagine new possibilities for herself and whether she could be the kind of person who buys this or that product.

As so often with shopping, however, there are nuances and contradictions below the level of the more overt building of relationships. For one thing, the fact that she has stressed that this will be a small shop, and he that it will be a large one, is not unconnected to the fact that it is her turn to pay the bill. Furthermore, as so often with love, the relationship that is being forged while shopping is not based on equality. Even within what appears to be a feminist middle-class relationship with a more experienced divorcee, they establish a clear asymmetry. In general, she is trying to develop a more intimate knowledge of him and his desires, while he is establishing that he has the final word in most decision-making. He vetoes choices such as a soyabean mix by saying he doesn't like soya, but I saw no cases of her vetoing him. They are both vegetarian but she sometimes eats fish. He wants them to end up with an agreement based on his preference, and manages to drop enough hints to make her say at one point 'Why do you keep going on about it?' As decisions accumulate it becomes clear that although she will permit an unequal relationship, this should not be so overt as to prevent her from finding ways to hide this fact from herself. In addition they both have other relationships of care to mark. He normally takes his mother shopping and here buys extra goods for her. She has her daughter to think about, and as so often buys goods which are slightly less 'junky' versions of those requested by her daughter. These are accompanied with the typical explanation that 'I would like to wean her onto something healthier.' Within a few weeks of this shopping expedition the couple informed me they were engaged.

Few opportunities arose to observe such 'shopping as courtship' expeditions. Apart from individuals, the single most common shopping genre was also the most fraught, which is when mothers shop with infants. Here the relationship between power and love becomes far more explicit, as do the contradictions of love. Mothers with babies are constantly torn between a sense of pride and desire to show off their infant to appreciative fellow shoppers and the anxiety that mounts as babies lose 'patience' and start to cry, struggle and embarrass their parents. Such ambivalence continues as toddlers express often unmitigated greed, negating the sense of innocence and nature that the parent would wish them to express.[13] This is also the most unambiguous relationship of love in that no amount of anxiety, frustration or embarrassment can undermine the fundamental belief that the relationship being expressed and developed in endless battles and compromises should be called love.

Around those varieties of love that remain clearly within a normative centre lie other examples that are both more problematic and in some cases better regarded as exceptions. Clary illustrates the problems that arise when relentless poverty becomes in and of itself a constraint to the expression of such sentiments. Clary is a single mother living in a council flat, who simply cannot manage on the meagre government support she receives. Her present hardship is exacerbated by having been caught without a television licence so that she is also paying off a fine. The father of her two children is much better off, and she feels particularly vulnerable because she simply cannot compete with his generosity when the children go and stay with him, and she is worried about the indulgences they become used to while there. In effect, her love is manifested largely as anxiety about shopping, rather than in shopping itself. The social science literature on consumption often seems to echo most journalism in making the daft assumption that it is mainly the rich who are materialistic. Clary, however, like most people I worked with who live in considerable poverty, is much more materialistic than the rich, because of the miserable consequences of her lack of goods. For Clary, this is reflected not merely in her persistent worrying about goods she cannot afford but the deeper sense that she is a failure as a mother as a result of this. These anxieties constantly surface in conversations as in a discussion about birthday parties for children at the school.

A Yeah Ruth has been to quite a few, and one of Mark's friends had to go to McDonalds, and it's really expensive, especially when there's about twelve or fourteen children, and I can't even afford to get Mark a birthday card let alone a party or anything.

I mean it's his birthday on Tuesday and he's gone down to their
[the father's] house for the week, so I mean I've only just sent a
card down. It's all I can afford. It's very difficult when you're on
your own and you haven't got any money, and I feel quite embarrassed when they have to keep going to parties, and I haven't
really got a present but I sort of manage to get something.

The same anxiety permeates the experience of shopping with
Clary. On one occasion – an extremely hot day – when we had
walked to the shopping centre to save on fares, the children start
to ask for drinks as soon as we arrive. I decide to buy ice lollies
for all four of us (I was pretty thirsty too!). But Clary is immediately nervous. Eating slows them down. The lollies melt before
they can be eaten properly and she has to hold her daughter's
lolly for her, and eat some of the looser ice cream to stop it
falling off. She then becomes upset about their sticky hands and
faces, and makes clear by various gestures that I should not have
bought them lollies – that she sort of knew that this is what
would happen. She then buys a pack of tissues she cannot afford
in order to clean the children up. Pride, love, guilt – one could
attach so many labels to Clary's feelings and actions (and add
insensitivity to mine). For most parents love is often subsumed
within anxiety, but for Clary anxiety is often about all she has.

The concept of making love in shopping is even more problematic when the issue is not one of lack of money, but lack of a
relationship to which love can be directed. In this particular area
there are two main varieties of single-person household. The first
and most numerous is that of the elderly. In general, these tend
also to be amongst the most impoverished households, occupying
the most run-down part of the council flats. There exist amongst
the elderly some of the most self-obsessed individuals in the street,
for example, one elderly male who had never married and clearly
regarded other people (in particular inquisitive anthropologists)
with considerable malevolence. Despite my perseverance in enquiry I could uncover very little beneath his armour of autonomy.
It should be said, however, that this individualism did not always
result in selfishness, and that he, along with a number of other
elderly persons, took part in the routine shopping for those

elderly in the flats who were invalids and unable to shop for themselves.

Many amongst the elderly show considerable ingenuity in turning shopping into acts of love for both their descendants and their ancestors. The former is more common, but will be discussed in detail below as part of the analysis of thrift. I will therefore instead provide an example of the latter. This involved an older (she would not like to have been called elderly) woman who clearly shopped incessantly as a means of keeping occupied. The problem then arose as to how to keep such shopping going when in reality she had little in the way of goods she needed and little by way of money to buy them. In practice she develops 'projects' which fortunately are very hard to come to fruition. Several of these relate to gifts she will have to buy for Christmas, a wedding or a christening that she can start thinking about months, even years ahead. A more elaborate project revolved around an ancestral shrine. This consisted of the decoration of the flat with photographs of her parents and other deceased relatives. So, for example, she needed a particular photo frame to match exactly one she already had, but which she could never find, combined with other elements such as the right artificial flowers that would festoon the portraits. Through such devices she manages to engage herself in daily acts of shopping where most of the time is spent considering others and maintaining the same subsumption of the self that was crafted through decades of housewifery, but now returns as affection for her ancestors.

The other major form of single-person household in this area is that of single professional women who have developed strong career aspirations aided by feminism, but have had difficulty in finding men they regard as equal to themselves. Quite often, however, as in the couple described shopping/courting together, even where they are not in established households they have relationships of various degrees on-going or on the horizon. Many of them seemed to have reached an age where their shopping is directed towards the imagined establishment of a household, though in practice this may well end up as a single-parent household. They are therefore closer to housewives than they are to the more clearly individualistic teenagers. Just as it should not be assumed that materialism is best associated with those who possess goods, so also it should not be assumed that it is the single person who is most individualistic. On the contrary, if anything it is the lonely who are more obsessed with relationships than those who can afford to take them for granted.

Perhaps most revealing of the problem of a lack of objects of love is Christine. She is a secretary and has few of the class and career aspirations of the dominant group of single women, and few aspirations with regard to partners either. Rather she has entered a cycle of mild depression that saps the confidence that would help her in either one of these aims. For those who see shopping as a vicarious activity, where interest in commodities replaces the search for social relations, she might well have been a candidate for intensive shopping. But as I argued with respect to an earlier study of kitchen decoration in North London (Miller 1988), the evidence is quite the contrary. Concern for particular goods tends to come from the development rather than from the absence of meaningful relationships. An inability to relate to people usually means an inability to relate to goods also. As such, Christine finds little pleasure in shopping. Her conversation is replete with statements such as 'I haven't shopped for clothes for ages' or

Q Do you like shopping?
A No not really! I used to. I've gone off it now. I'm trying to decorate so I've been looking for furniture and that's just been awful.

Or

A I don't like shopping for food because it's too heavy to carry back. No I don't really enjoy the shopping, not at the moment, but that's probably my frame of mind at the moment, I'm not really interested in that sort of thing.

The only exception is when she can shop with a female friend, a shopping companion of ten years' standing – and then there is her cat. On several occasions the conversation also meanders wistfully back to a time when she did enjoy shopping, when there was some point to it.

There are, however, those for whom the generalizations I intend to develop on the basis of such material would not hold. Teenagers are certainly 'other' directed, but the other is often mainly a mirror (both literally and figuratively) in which they wish to gain a better sense of who they are. While they may talk of love rather more easily than their elders, they are less likely to conform to that version of love being described here. They may well be the group which comes closest to the conventional vision of shopping as devoted to the development of individual identity. There were cases of married women who could by no stretch of the imagination be seen as largely subsuming their own desires within service to their partners. There were relationships that were breaking up or where shopping was used to manifest rivalry and jealousy. Mary, one such exception, will be introduced later on. But even taken together these amount to a minority perspective held against a norm of shopping as an expression of care and concern.

To conclude: the ethnographic evidence has been used to re-direct attention from shopping as an expression of individual subjectivity and identity to an expression of kinship and other relationships. It could be argued that it is misleading to talk of making love, when one has here such a variety of relationships but this would be to ignore the crucial role of ideology in legitimating these relationships. As one listens to and takes part in the practice of these relationships it becomes clear that it is almost forbidden to understand or justify any dyadic formation except in the context of love. Parents are well aware of their responsibilities to their children and even of their legal requirements, but they would be highly offended by the suggestion that these alone are the cause of their devotion. Couples may have individual interests at stake and conflicts in practice, but they present the situation to themselves as founded on love, without which their relationship not only could but should be ended. Siblings and friends are understood to be cared for with more reason than obligation or reciprocity. Love is essential because it asserts the ideal of agency within any given relationship. What is rejected is any language of obligation that suggests we maintain relationships solely out of enforced behaviour. To define a relationship in any terms other than love seems to be taken as a debasement of that relationship.[14]

The Anthropologist beyond Voyeurism

Anthropologists tend to conduct an analysis by expanding the context within which a particular practice can be considered. Shopping for groceries is not an isolated activity but one that takes its place within a much wider cycle of activities and concerns. For supermarket shopping the most immediate context is providing meals for oneself or for a family. I recently read in sequence two books about this activity. The first is called *The Making and the Unmaking of the Haya Lived World* and is by Brad Weiss (1996) and the other is *Feeding the Family* by Marjorie DeVault (1991).

Weiss's study is based in Tanzania, and concerns the cosmology of the Haya as constituted within what the author calls the phenomenology of everyday activities. The emphasis is on cooking as an activity linking growing or buying foods and then preparing them for feeding the family. Weiss shows how much of the wider cosmology of the Haya is encapsulated in the particular discourses of cooking and feeding. His analysis provides profound insights into the complex web of metaphors and symbolism that constitute a set of values developed over a considerable period. For example, he explores the relationship between certain foodstuffs associated with males and stored around the hearth, and the female role in processing these on the hearth to make them edible. The distinctions are partly expressed through attributes such as moisture that also have connotations of sexuality.

Weiss then shows how the same symbolic system evolves in dynamic tension with recent innovations such as shopping and new transport systems that are conceptually and practically integrated within Haya cosmology, though often objectified as pathologies such as 'plastic teeth extraction' or 'electric vampires'. Such innovations are related back to cooking and food preparation processes which, as the Haya perceive it, slow down the world to an encompassable pace of life and lifeworlds. It is the sheer complexity and interwoven nature of cosmology based on countless metaphors and associations, that creates a habitus that entraps modernity and renders the experience of new goods and opportunities specific to the Haya.

This is high-quality ethnography analysed in terms largely familiar to anthropologists. It is also strikingly different from the book *Feeding the Family* (DeVault 1991), which is written by a feminist sociologist with reference to urban United States. The distinction lies not so much in what the Haya or Americans do. It becomes impossible to compare these directly because of the extreme differences in the way the material is approached and analysed. DeVault's book is also an analysis of superb quality. It represents one of the most thorough-going investigations to come out of the tradition that arose early on in feminist studies of uncovering the work involved in being a housewife within the domestic world. I know of no other research that so effectively makes explicit the endless endeavours of housewifery, the constant juggling of care and consideration as one learns about and tries to deal with the needs and desires of several other persons at the same time. The book is particularly effective in going beyond merely observing the labour involved. It gives equal weight to the huge effort of consciousness involved in planning, considering and taking account of the complex and often contradictory demands made upon the housewife. DeVault discusses shopping, but the emphasis is on shopping as a stage in the preparing and giving of meals to the family.

The evidence provided by her study seems almost entirely compatible with the descriptions I have given of shopping. DeVault provides considerable evidence to show that the bulk of decision-making is orientated to others, and involves constant self-sacrifice by the housewife. She notes 'in contrast to the responsiveness to the tastes of others, most women were scrupulously careful not to give their own preferences any special weight . . . "one of us has to compromise, and it's going to end up being me"'

(1991: 43). Also, as in my own ethnography, this housewifery is much more than merely reflecting the desires of other members of the household. It is also seen as an educative and transforming means by which these others can be developed and moulded according to the wider aspirations that form part of the house-wives' concern and care.

DeVault is quite clear about the radical disjuncture between her perspective on these activities and those of most of her informants: 'Many women spoke of doing work they did not enjoy in order to please their husbands. However, very few of them expressed explicit discomfort about these efforts, and only those described above reported any sustained, overt conflict with their husbands. I was puzzled and a bit dismayed by their complacency about what I saw as inequity' (1991: 156).

DeVault's task is constantly to re-evaluate all that she observed in terms of the work or effort involved. The term 'inequity' is directly related to what she sees as asymmetry or lack of equivalence. DeVault is then four-square behind the modernist project of equality in which a key component is to reduce cultural practice to some sense of equivalence where inequalities are thereby made clear and explicit.

By contrast, Brad Weiss in his analysis of the Haya does none of these things. His concern is to demonstrate the moral and cosmological worlds that are objectified in feeding the family. There is no sense of an adjudication between the social agents in terms of how things ought to be different from the way they are. As a foreign anthropologist Weiss does not have the temerity to pronounce upon his ethnographic informants and define them as wrong, while DeVault as an insider would clearly consider it iniquitous to do anything else. But there is another equally important difference in the style of the accounts. DeVault's informants constantly talk about love and care. The Haya either don't or Weiss does not report it. DeVault's own ideology of effort and equality exists in clear tension with the other side of this modernist context which is a discourse of love. Indeed DeVault is so concerned to emphasize this discrepancy that she pays little attention to the difference between care and love directed to the children (which she might otherwise have defended) and an ideology of love which hides the efforts being made on behalf of husbands (to which she maintains a critical stance).

My project in this essay is to follow the more conventional anthropological approach exemplified by Weiss rather than that of DeVault.[15] The question I seek to address is whether shopping may reveal, amongst other things, a generalizable cosmology, and if so what that reveals about the cosmological beliefs of contemporary peoples in North London. I am well aware that, such is the lack of community and the diversity of the households on the street, this is not a reasonable expectation, but, of course, I write with *déjà vu*, that is the belief that normativity is exactly what I have discovered. Equally, love is not to be taken for granted as the context for shopping. In the third chapter a brief examination will be made of the historical conditions which gave rise to this centrality of love in the self-legitimation of these practices. It will not be surprising to discover that it has arisen in dialectical tension with the modernist ideals of equality and exchange which here are used to condemn it as an obfuscation of the truth of contemporary relationships.

This is also the reason why almost all the examples given are those of female shoppers. The ethnography included single men (especially elderly males) and some households where shopping was divided fairly equally between men and women. There are also goods such as car parts, alcohol and Do-it-Yourself where shopping is dominated by males. Yet in most cases it was clear that even when men are heavily involved there is a strong tendency to distance themselves from identification with the act and the concept of shopping. Even the exceptions amongst feminist-influenced males who do positively identify with shopping tend to see this as precisely a feminist act (I would place myself in this category). They experience their shopping as a deliberate form of positive discrimination for which they expect to obtain (and almost always actually receive) far more credit than would a female who merely shops out of conformity to traditional expectations. Much is revealed by this difference in the treatment of the male and female shopper. The female shopper is ideologically inscribed as the norm, irrespective of the statistics that demonstrate a diversity of practice. It follows that an essay on the foundational cosmology of shopping will be primarily concerned with the female shopper.

Finally, it should be noted that the excavation of exploitation in housewifery is merely one strand within a much wider set of academic and political projects created by feminism. In chapter 3 the anthropologist Annette Weiner will be used to exemplify another quest, which is to uncover the positive values that may be harboured within the normative ideologies[16] that have become established as specifically feminine in particular times and places. These tend to be more fully explored in research on topics such as gender and sexuality. Here, questions are raised about whether attributes such as trust and sensitivity have been themselves gendered and what strategies might be used to transcend such dualism and make them more general attributes of human relationships.

The Treat

It is an essential part of this theory that there exists a normative expectation that most shoppers will subordinate their personal desires to a concern for others, and that this will be implicitly legitimated as love. As is often the case the norm is perhaps best determined by focusing upon the exception that defines it, in this case the treat. Almost any substantial shopping expedition incorporated both the concept and the practice of the treat. Although (as will be seen) the treat varies considerably in its usage, in most cases the treat is an element of shopping that is directed at a particular individual and is thereby excepted from the rest of the shopping where that is understood as being on behalf of the household as a whole. Furthermore the treat is usually regarded as an extra extravagance that lies outside the constraints of necessity, thrift or moderation that binds together most mundane provisioning. My argument is that the treat by its existence defines the rest of shopping for the shopper as not a treat, i.e. as directed to necessity, to moderation and as on behalf of some larger entity.

This interpretation is not given by the shoppers themselves, who have not usually ever discussed or reflected upon the treat *per se*. Yet it is an implication which can easily be drawn out. An examination of the treat may begin by returning to Mrs Wynn, who remains typical with respect to this as to other aspects of her shopping.

A Yes I always do, just get myself something. If it's last week it was just some different biscuits that I kept away and I got a melon. They were on offer, I love melon. It would be a yoghurt, especially if I do it over the weekend, or a bar of chocolate. I can't do it for nothing! Actually I've never thought of it that way but now your saying that, yes, I obviously go around thinking what am I going to get for myself, and that's what I do, but now you've actually highlighted it.
Q Is the treat earned?
A Yes definitely. The week before my sister was up and I got a big bar of chocolate for the both of us and I did get some ice cream.
Q Do you eat it before you get back?
A No. I hide them in the back of the cupboard because Jack can't get up there anyway.
Q When do you have it?
A When I'm on my own or in the evening or something.

The idea that the treat is a direct reward to the shopper for carrying out the act of shopping is a very common one. It is more usual for the treat to be consumed before the shopper returns to the house, though for those shoppers who do tend to bring the treat home, they like Mrs Wynn tend to start by hiding it. Commonly the treat is also understood as a slightly transgressive purchase, something fattening or sweet as well as expensive for what it is. Often the treat was observed as a practice but not spoken of unless elicited in questions such as:

Q Do you buy yourself a treat when food shopping?
A Yes I might buy a gateau or, I don't actually like sweet things that much anyway, that would be about it, or maybe avocados.
Q What about for your husband?
A Well usually the boys raid the bags when I get home anyway, but if I've managed to pack it away before they come home, I present something basically as a treat.

Q Anything particular for your husband?
A Well I'm not a great meat eater so I would probably buy him a piece of steak, which I really wouldn't want to, so that would be it.

The treat may be used to individualize any family member as the recipient of a special purchase, but it is most commonly phrased as a reward for the shopper. This reward element is also a major factor in another common form of treat, which was something given to children for agreeing to be good while shopping (or having been good while at home). Apart from the poorest mothers, such treats are a constant feature of grocery shopping with children, and most parents would find it hard to imagine shopping accompanied by children without such treats. Many of these treats are eaten before they even reach the check-out, so that they are paid for using the empty wrappers. Children also commonly help themselves to sweets and other goods which simply appear in the trolley when the parent is not looking. No parent had a consistent response to this. They may be either put back or allowed as a treat depending on the mood of the shopper and the current state of the relationship, parent to child. Curiously, there is also an extremely common practice amongst adults of eating one or more grapes soon after entering the supermarket, as a kind of treat taken from the supermarket itself. A high proportion of shoppers do this, and few shoppers were observed to eat any other commodity without paying.

For children, the treat is often merely the feeling that their mother, who has had largely to ignore them in the labour of provisioning, grants them both attention and time. Several parents described a variety of toy-shop visiting in these terms. There is a clear understanding that such visits should not involve any purchase of toys. The child is allowed some time to wander around looking at toys, or in those shops such as The Early Learning Centre which permit it, also to play with toys. This becomes a time which individualizes their concerns within the more general task of shopping as provisioning. Another treat for children may take the form of eating out while shopping. At least for middle-class shoppers this has become an established norm, and usually involves a visit to a fast-food outlet such as a hamburger joint.

In one case it is merely buying a special sticky bun whenever they pass a bakery. Most children are quite adept at turning what starts as a treat into a ritual, in the sense that this becomes an invariant element in all subsequent shopping expeditions.

Eating out is also understood as a treat in the sense of a personal indulgence for the shopper. So even a shopper who claims to rarely have treats, notes in response to a question about treats that she may, on occasion, stop at a particular store for a cup of coffee. For many others, eating out is a much more important element. For middle-class shoppers the cafeterias attached to some of the more up-market department stores are the preferred sites for such treats. For many families, to eat out is itself a treat, quite apart from any relation to shopping. For the housewife, in particular, the treat element may be represented as a release from the work involved in cooking for the family. A common argument over the booking of holidays is the tension between the relative lack of expense of self-catering and the housewife's feeling that this would diminish her right to holidays as leisure time.

The shop that is itself most commonly associated with the concept of the treat is Marks & Spencer. It also played a conspicuous role in creating a bridge between the treat as an element of shopping and the treat as a more generic category for families. This involved a particular act of symbolic substitution repeated by a number of middle-class families with young children. With very few exceptions, the evaluation of the Marks & Spencer food supermarkets remains constant. It is viewed as having far and away the best range of foods from the point of view of taste and it is regarded as equally distinguished by its high prices. The use of this shop for regular groceries is relatively rare. Instead, the shop emerged as being symbolically as much related to the category of restaurant as to that of supermarket. Marks & Spencer pioneered the art of own-label pre-prepared meals in Britain and it is this type of food for which it is chiefly known. The pattern that has become established is that young couples who used to eat out at restaurants on, say a weekly basis, now shop at Marks & Spencer for a meal which they will eat at home as a direct substitute for going out to a restaurant. This is a result of their need to stay in with the children. A housewife readily noted that

A Yes, I actually see ready meals as treats too because it's a treat for me actually coming home from work to be able to just stick something in the oven.

Another suggested:

A Marks & Spencer is a treat for us. It's our weekend treat. If we are not going out, which we can't much anyway. Definitely, because beforehand we used to eat out a lot, so it's the next best thing is having the microwave do it for you.

In such cases although it is the couple that is treated, the wife is especially marked as not having to cook. Husbands are less commonly the recipients of a treat as against the shopper or the child, but they are often selected as the individual who should purchase the treats. This follows from the division of shopping labour that, as feminist research has clearly shown, creates the woman as the person whose desires are subsumed in the labour of provisioning and the man as the person whose personal desires can and should be expressed and indulged in shopping. It is common then for the male partner to be regarded as the natural provider of special indulgences which by the same token then valorizes the work of the housewife as provider.

The degree of collusion in this use of gender as difference is evident in the case of Michelle.

A Well, I think he doesn't do the shopping very often and when he does he tends to be more indulgent. I tend to think more about the money side of things. Like for example when he was on his half-term break, he did the shopping one day and he bought lots of what I would call indulgent things that I wouldn't normally buy. But he only does it because he doesn't shop very often. I think if he was doing the shopping regularly then he wouldn't . . .

Well, the thing was when it was half-term break I knew he'd be going shopping and I knew he would come home with these things so I was sort of expecting them in a way. And if he came home just buying staple foods I would have wondered how come he didn't buy anything else like that.

In a wealthier household, the husband tends to buy food mainly at a delicatessen, which is often seen as a shop specifically for treats. He also buys clothes for his wife as treats. This is the most common use of gender distinctions but the opposite scenario was also found. Where it is the woman who is regarded as more self-indulgent, then the husband is likely to take on the opposed role as keeper of fiscal responsibility. Here, the wife may feel guilty when she fails to share her treat, since she tends to eat and drink whatever is around, while he would tend to store things up for special occasions (that may not actually arise).

A Then of course it's unfair on James because then there's no biscuits, 'cos I can't live with the biscuit tin. So when he wants a biscuit there never is one. So what I do is I buy him the type he likes and I go upstairs and I put them in the cupboard.

The same husband at one point becomes rather concerned when he feels the wife is going too far in treating herself so that rewards become, from his point of view, self-indulgence.

A Just after I had Charles, James and I went shopping together and I bought myself about five treats, and this was sort of a subject of some arguments. Like a packet of these particular biscuits I like or a slightly more expensive wine. I do remember I bought, I had to admit afterwards, although I wouldn't have admitted it in the argument we had, that it was true I had gone slightly over the top with this reward treating myself. I just said 'look I've just had a baby' . . . James is happier if I keep the overall bill down, that's his treat when I don't treat myself or him or Charles or whatever.

In this case the wife acknowledges her overspending. More commonly in such situations, a woman will judge for herself what she sees as the reasonable reward for her labours, in terms of a balance with his expenditures, and if necessary hide such deserved treats from her husband, as one notes:

A I have friends who hide clothes from their partners and when they bring it out of the cupboard and their partner says 'Is that new?' they say 'No I've had it for ages', and occasionally I have resorted to that! He doesn't see me as extravagant, but he knows I like spending money. Whatever I spend is always minimal in comparison to him as he is into computers.

In this case, however, the concern is moving from a treat *per se* to more general issues about the control of expenditure within the household.[17] Although I am mainly considering supermarket shopping, this example also shows that the same point about treats would follow from clothes shopping. Most women regard the clothes they buy as requirements (to a far greater extent than the journalistic representation of shopping would allow), but will point to the various clothing items that were also purchased as treats, which is likely to imply both extravagance and the lack of any immediate need for the garment.

If the treat demonstrates that the rest of shopping is not self-directed, it must follow that the treat itself is. The concept of the treat thereby throws open various questions about the nature of the self. The word 'treat' seems to evoke not just the idea of extravagance but also foods that are fattening. The following response is therefore not surprising in relation to the idea of a treat:

A I might buy myself something if I'm not on a diet. I think 'Oh stuff it, I know it's wrong, but I'm going to have it.' Every week it's going to be this week for the diet but the only specific product I buy is soup to take to work. I may have a week when I buy natural yoghurt but, it doesn't last, and I'll make sure we're well stocked on salads, things that are tempting on the healthy front. The children would still have their bits and pieces so it would not affect them.

This tension also provides an insight into a very familiar form of shopping behaviour, which is the idea of shopping itself as a treat to be carried out when depressed. Indeed, the items purchased when depressed, such as a book for an academic, chocolate for the food shopper, cosmetics or an accessory for younger women, are precisely the kinds of item that are also purchased as treats. Though not often brought up in conversation, this behaviour is readily acknowledged when prompted. Although this is more usually an individual activity it can apply to a couple:

A We always say we bought that CD player when we were feeling depressed. Because Alfred had just snapped his Achilles tendon, had his foot in plaster, and our car had just rolled down a hill in Ibis Pond[18] car park and smashed into four others. It had a faulty handbrake, and we went out and bought something to cheer us up.

This may also involve collective action as in the following quotation from a middle-class female:

A I've done that in the past, yeah. I have done that before when I lived with my flatmate when I was in college. I think it's always different when you just live with girlfriends anyway. They enjoy shopping much more when it's a bunch of girls, and we would go 'My god I'm really fed up, lets go shopping, and I need some shoes, and come along you can find something to buy as well', and we'd go and we'd both get a pair of shoes, or get our hair cut or whatever and feel a lot better. Completely superficial things but it was nice, it made a nice fun thing. We'd say 'Oh I'm really pissed off this week, we deserve to go', and we'd do that.

The treat works well as a direct response to depression because it is an action which specifically reaffirms the self. It alleviates a condition where the shopper feels specifically disregarded (if only by fate!), by an act of indulgence that reconfirms the special nature of the recipient of this purchase. Because the treat becomes the linchpin in associating consumption with the self, it is perhaps a useful route to understanding those pathologies in which the self becomes obsessively directed to the ambiguities of treating as in the relationship of bulimics and anorexics to items such as chocolate and cream cakes.

Under more typical conditions the main role of the treat is in respect to the housewife in her routine provisioning, where the self is particularly unacknowledged. It will also serve for many other selves (or larger social units), where appropriate. Even when understood to be a reward for labour, the treat is also clearly regarded as a hedonistic act of materialistic self-indulgence. The treat thereby conforms to journalistic generalizations about shopping in general. But very few people attempt to make shopping into constant treating. For the vast majority the treat is the exceptional and special act of indulgence that thereby defines the rest of shopping as anything but a treat. In short, if shopping were all a treat, the shopper wouldn't feel the need to have a treat *per se*.

The treat then is an important piece of evidence behind the suggestion that most shopping is directed to people other than the shoppers themselves. In some cases the treat is offered to the household as a whole, for example, when the family goes out for a meal. In this and in the case of a Marks & Spencer substitute for the meal out, it is the element of extravagance and special occasion which is being drawn out through conceptualizing the activity as a treat. As a 'frame' in Goffman's (1975) sense, the treat then brands all non-treat expenditure as mundane provisioning where the opposite criteria should apply.

The more common result is the individualizing of the recipient of the treat as against the more generic provisioning of households. This is a particularly subtle discrimination when it comes to the shopper herself. It is quite clear that there is a class of treats that is judged to be a reward for her labour in having undertaken the shopping. But why should this then come to be regarded as a treat? Obviously people do not regard wages and other justified rewards for labour as treats. This only makes sense because shopping is understood to be a labour that unlike waged labour is done by housewives as an expression of something that transcends the logic of exchange. Furthermore, a shopper from a single-person household will still regard her- or himself as buying a special purchase as a treat by which they are individualized. This provides further evidence against the supposition that single persons are necessarily more individualistic.

The treat conflates the act of separating out the individual from the household with the act of separating out extravagance from the normative ethos of shopping, which is thrift. That which the shopper does on behalf of the household is governed by thrift, while their individual presence is signified by the treat.

This suggests that an investigation of thrift as the opposite of the treat will help provide a further stage towards a conceptualization of that larger entity which is understood as the proper recipient of shopping. What is this 'household' which transcends the individuals and dyadic relationships out of which it is constituted, even when the household consists of a single person?

Thrift

The treat is usually a minor element in any particular shopping expedition, most often a single item that is whipped into the shopping trolley quickly so as to be hardly noticed by the shopper themselves. By contrast, by far the most important activity in the experience of shopping, apart from actually bringing back the items purchased, is saving. Also, by contrast, saving is a highly explicit, often debated and constantly foregrounded element in shopping. It will be shown that the variety of ways in which a sense of saving can enter into the shopping expedition is quite extraordinary. It will also be found that saving as an experience is by no means the same thing as actually spending less money, and that its purpose within shopping is by no means as straightforward as might have been anticipated. In a theoretical analysis towards the end of this essay I will suggest that thrift is best understood not, as one might suppose, as a means towards some other end, but rather as an end in itself.

During the ethnography it was possible to encounter what I had imagined to be the classic experience of saving: the specific search for lower prices based on systematic comparative shopping. The most common practitioners of this art tend to be the elderly. Mrs Lloyd may serve as an example. Mrs Lloyd is eighty-four years old and lives with her husband, all of whose working life was spent in retail. She had recently had a knee operation and was being helped to the supermarket by her daughter, who was in her fifties and had travelled a considerable distance in order to be with her mother. Mrs Lloyd uses the trolley to support herself while going around the shop. For Mrs Lloyd the primary aim of shopping is to search out 'specials', that is products that have been marked down from their usual price. She had already been told about certain specials by a friend of hers who had been in the same shop a couple of days before, and her first disappointment comes when she finds that the 'red label' tea she is looking for had been returned to its regular price. She does not buy it.

Almost every item is subject to explicit debate. The main comparisons are made with the supermarket where her daughter lives, since Mrs Lloyd expects her daughter to have memorized the price of all relevant items, and her daughter rarely fails her. The other comparison is with a particular greengrocer, Tom's, that has an almost legendary status in the street. Although it is situated in Ibis Pond, which is generally an expensive shopping area, this particular shop has far and away the cheapest fruit and vegetables in the area, cheaper than any of the market stalls. Apart from price comparison, Mrs Lloyd needs to inspect the particular package. For example, after consideration she chooses the Little Gem lettuce hearts at a higher price than a whole lettuce, since she reasons that the relative lack of waste makes them better value. At one point the daughter finds a special which was not present in her own area and buys it. The most anxious period of the shopping expedition comes as a result of the development of metric weights and measures. This transition is only partial, and Mrs Lloyd finds that when she wants to compare two packages of frozen lamb, one is in pounds and the other is in kilos. She finds this extremely frustrating and engages in conversation with her neighbouring shopper about the confusion such things cause. Mrs Lloyd is not at all convinced that things will be much better when everything goes metric, since she feels she is too old a dog to learn new tricks. Nevertheless, while in the supermarket she does pick up a leaflet on metrification to take home with her. Generally she tends to buy supermarket own brand goods, but at one point she is faced with Andrex brand toilet rolls. She first notes that these have gone up in price considerably, but then her daughter observes the shelf label which gives the price per 100 grams. She calculates that there is such a saving on the pack of twelve that this would work out cheaper than the own brand toilet rolls, so Mrs Lloyd buys the Andrex.

Altogether Mrs Lloyd buys twenty-three items, of which twenty were the subject of specific discussion based on price comparison. After this the daughter goes on separately to Tom's for the fruit and vegetables, while I return home with Mrs Lloyd.

Within the ethnography as a whole there was only one younger woman who had anything like this level of knowledge about individual prices. Indeed, the astonishing finding was rather how few people, at any income level, knew the prices of most basic goods. Many shoppers could only just manage the price of bread and milk, items they buy several times a week, and there were some who did not even get this far. When it comes to less commonly purchased goods few shoppers have much idea of price. This is notwithstanding the development of various television shows such as 'The Price is Right' which have belatedly valorized this particular element of shopping skill. This lack of price knowledge does not, however, prevent an emphasis upon thrift which rivals the concern exhibited by Mrs Lloyd. There are new forms of bargain hunting which have been facilitated by developments in supermarket presentation and fully exploited by shoppers. The major supermarkets are extremely efficient retailers who in Britain have an overwhelming dominance of food retailing. Although I will be focusing upon the shopper's perspective, the evidence for the centrality of thrift to shopping is equally evident from the way supermarkets have facilitated this possibility. The new forms of bargain hunting cannot be understood outside the context of retail strategies.[19]

The first and most important element of thrift in supermarket shopping is the search for savers. The 'saver' is a generic term here for a number of different kinds of bargain. The most recent form of saver is the 'value' version of the supermarkets' own-label goods. Each supermarket has its own name for this range, and they are packaged in conspicuously different ways; for example, Kwiksave uses pure white, Tesco a distinctive blue and white stripe. These are literally no-frills packages. They often cost considerably less than the ordinary own-label brand. The value line represents a point in a gradation for most products that starts with the key brands as the most expensive version and passes through own-label goods which thereby become mid-price versions. The concept of the own-label supermarket brand has gone further in Britain than in most other countries.[20] Major supermarket firms such as Sainsbury may have up to 8,000 own-label brands (Doel 1996: 50). These are usually, though not invariably, cheaper than the normal branded goods, so that choosing them over the other brand itself represents an act of saving.

The second kind of saver is the type that Mrs Lloyd goes in search of, which is the product that is marked down for a limited period. One generalization that seemed to hold throughout the year's fieldwork was that this kind of saver was the single most important reason why shoppers altered their intentions and purchased an item not originally on their shopping list. Indeed, the entire weight of advertising seemed virtually inconsequential by comparison. There were few instances of a clear desire to buy a product as a result of advertising, but it was very rare to take part in a supermarket expedition that was not transformed in the light of savers, even for those shoppers who professed not to be interested in them.

This kind of saver has its own sub-varieties. An inspection of a Safeway supermarket in Wood Green revealed a supermarket strategy based on a combination of colours and shapes that allowed certain labels to stand out from the main. These included goods marked down from the previous week and goods with offers such as 'buy three for the price of two'. Other savers were based on the advantage of buying the larger item. Indeed in some cases there was no actual claim made for any kind of reduction, simply a label called 'price watch', which by virtue of having the same colours and motifs as the other saver goods appeared by implication to indicate a saving which may not have actually been the case. I have little doubt that this device made many shoppers buy goods in the mistaken belief that this was a price reduction. In many product ranges between a fifth and a quarter of lines were represented by some kind of special label that either was or implied a saving. This surely says a great deal about the importance of this technique. Indeed, it is hard to imagine that a supermarket could go much beyond an implied saving on twenty-five per cent of its lines without making the whole concept of saving devalued beyond acceptable plausibility to the shopper.

The evidence of accompanied shopping is that these savers are highly successful.

From the perspective of the shopper, the saver is only one, if the most important, element in the experience of thrift achieved by scanning supermarket shelves for all the examples of any particular product. Where a shopper is choosing between value label, own-label and branded goods, the equation to be made is between price and perceived quality. Most shoppers do not buy value labels. When challenged they are likely to suggest that this is because the quality of 'cheap' goods is so low as to be poor value. As well as price against quality, shoppers these days are almost always faced with a simultaneous choice of price against quantity, in as much as most goods may be bought in greater bulk at a lower price. The effect is that the size of the package may again be understood as a saving. Finally, the major supermarkets facilitate this decision making by adding in small letters on each label the price per weight. The result is that most purchases revolve around the simultaneous computation of three intersecting equations, which will provide a choice of goods directly in terms of money spent.[21]

One reason why there is such a wide range of goods is that there is a wide range of shoppers and clearly every one of these possible combinations is chosen by some section of the shopping market. But because each becomes, in effect, an equation between different parameters such as quality and price, virtually all shoppers, whichever strategy they choose to follow, can legitimate that choice on the grounds that they have made a saving. Either they have saved by buying a larger item, or an own-label/ value brand item, or they have bought the more expensive item because it is better quality, which thereby represents better value, or even a smaller item so that the surplus is not wasted. In short, it seems that the greater the permutations by which commerce supplies the goods the greater the permutations by which the shoppers legitimate their practice as a saving. For this purpose, the shoppers no longer need to have any knowledge taken from outside the shopping experience. They need to remember no information about prices in order to understand themselves to be practising thrift. All they need to do is to make the choice at the point of selection and justify that choice to themselves as a saving. This is precisely what most of them do most of the time.

Complex though it might seem, this act of supermarket shopping only scratches the surface of the gamut of possibilities by which shoppers may engage in bargain hunting and ensure that thrift is expressed through the act of spending. The logic that has been applied here to goods within a shop applies also to the choice between shops. Supermarkets are ranged clearly into high- and low-price stores. There is no doubt that shops such as Kwiksave and Poundstretcher will work out cheaper than the mainstream supermarkets such as Tesco and Sainsbury, which in turn are clearly outpriced by Marks & Spencer. The decision is again between price and perceived quality, since most shoppers assume that they get from these shops a quality equivalent to the price paid. Similarly, there is a choice based on quantity, in that for most goods these days there are bulk-buying facilities, which although not widely patronized are becoming more common.

The possibilities of thrift are extended greatly when one moves from the formal shops to the myriad other possibilities for purchase. There are many outlets that will claim low prices on the basis of low overheads. Within the high street, Argos makes this an explicit claim through having most of its goods in store rather than on show and then letting the shopper choose from a catalogue. In addition, there are many forms of thrift shop. Wood Green, which is the main shopping centre for people from this street, also has at least four different kinds of market stall. There is a 'market section' within the covered shopping centre, as well as individual stalls in the main thoroughfares of that centre. Outside, there is again a formal market area on certain days of the week, and several regular market stalls in other parts of the high street on almost every day of the week.

In addition to commodities and to shops, there is the factor of shop sales. Sales have become an ubiquitous feature of shopping. There have for many decades been the major seasonal sales, such as after Christmas, when virtually all shops have a clearing out of stock. These days there is also usually a summer sale and sometimes now a pre-Christmas or other sale. There are shops that have periodic sales and other shops such as Dixons that use the motif of the sale but make this a permanent feature of their presentation to the public. As far as shoppers are concerned they will look for particular sales for certain items.

A I had been waiting for the sales to buy her dresses in a boutique, a shop called Rainbow, their sale is really good.

Many, though by no means all, will also treat seasonal sales as a major element in their general purchasing strategy.

A Last year I bought a bed for John in the Selfridges sale which was really worth waiting for, and we went up to M&S in the West End and got suits for Brian on the first day – as they walk off the rails in minutes. That was a strategy, and we had a blow-out on that one post-Christmas sale. We tend to do that every couple of years, we needed specific things last year, this year we don't.

Others are less strategic and simply enjoy going to the sales *per se*. These are the shoppers who tend to feel they may have saved money on individual items but overall have spent more money than they should have done or indeed would otherwise have done as a result of going to sales.

A You have saved money in the sense that they were in the sale, but then again you buy more because the more you buy the more you save.

Complementing the fieldwork I carried out is Alison Clarke's parallel project based on the same households but looking at alternative forms of provisioning. In some cases, such as Tupperware parties, it would be hard to claim that prices are lower than in formal shops (although the party-givers try astonishingly hard to talk of value in terms of the longevity of the stock). The bulk of alternative provisioning is, however, based on the idea of saving money. Particularly important will be shopping through catalogues, participation at car boot sales, visits to other kinds of second-hand shops and stalls, including jumble sales, going to auctions to look for bargains, the use of *Loot* (or *Exchange and Mart*) catalogues which are specifically for the sale of second-hand goods and many other forms of alternative provisioning which she is documenting (e.g. Clarke 1997). Money is also saved by home-grown products, such as the use of allotments, home-brew distilling or sewing and making clothes.

To reiterate, mere inspection of the infrastructure of provisioning would tell one, even without any study of the shoppers themselves, that the sense of saving or thrift is the paramount concern within the activity of buying goods. Once one includes the direct study of the shoppers there appears in addition to these facilities, a wide range of strategies through which shoppers are able to see themselves as saving money. There are contexts in which bargaining or haggling occurs. There is the shopper who avoids bigger supermarkets where she thinks she will spend too much, and who in addition takes a basket instead of a trolley in order to purchase less. There is the shopper who sends her husband with a list, since he is so uninterested in shopping that he will not be tempted by the various extra items which would have seduced her. Taken together these provide a conclusion, that it is possible for shoppers to regard virtually the whole of the shopping expedition and the purchase of almost any specific item within that expedition, not as an act of spending at all, but as an act of saving. On many occasions I have returned to the home with a shopper to reflect on the shopping done. The conversation would not be of the form, 'I spent three pounds on beef' and 'I spent ten pounds on a bra' but of the form, 'look I saved fifty pence on ice cream' and 'I saved six pounds on my daughter's shoes.'

The factor of thrift should not be separated from its context, since quite often shoppers are trading off a concern to save money against other factors such as status. Furthermore, thrift is contextualized within a raft of concerns to do with proper behaviour. The pride in thrift is rarely merely an instrumental measurement of savings. It is also about a reticence towards expenditure in general with connotations of restraint, sobriety and respectability. Bragging about savings may be unseemly when thrift comes from the same stock of manners as modesty and an aversion to excess. For many of these households, thrift is also contextualized in a particular configuration of behaviours that have been stereotyped as British reticence and reserve.[22]

In a separate publication I have compared two shopping strategies related to thrift (Miller et al. in press). The first is the use of the price promise by the major department store John Lewis and the second the use of end-of-lease shops called cheapjacks along Wood Green high street. The point of that analysis was to demonstrate that there is a systematic opposition between the values objectified in these two sites which sheds considerable light on the nature and continued importance of class differences in shopping. John Lewis has established itself as expressive of a series of values such as rationalism and functionalism. Shoppers therefore trust it to provide a balance between price and quality that is termed good value. By contrast, cheapjacks which in some way parody the department store with their eclectic array of diverse categories of goods, try to imply that their piled-up bargains allow the consumer to profit from some semi-legal avoidance of the normal channels of provision.

From the point of view of the concerns of this essay, both could equally well be understood as strategies based on thrift. But in one case the image of thrift is saturated with middle-class notions of respectability and research, and in the other case thrift becomes part of a romance of working-class resistance to the establishment. It is possible therefore for thrift to be as powerful a factor for either class, and yet by being manifested through different strategies nevertheless demonstrates the clear symbolic opposition between the classes. Many middle-class shoppers will patronize second-hand and charity clothing shops that working-class shoppers would not dream of using, but the same middle-class shoppers would have considerable difficulty using supermarkets such as Kwiksave and Poundstretcher and show some reluctance even to use the value brands at shops they do identify with such as Tesco. The following quote comes from someone from a working-class background but currently moving up in the world:

A Yes, it is pride in a way. I often wonder how it would be if I was, say, looking through second-hand clothes in Oxfam [a charity shop] and I met somebody that I used to work with. And I think that probably would affect my pride. But it's never happened. But having said that, if I buy something in the second-hand shop,

I tend to be very pleased with it, and I say to my husband, 'Oh look, I picked this up in the second-hand shop.'

The trade-off between price and quality is also important here. There were not many shoppers who patronized the most expensive West End shops, but for those who did there was no suggestion that this represented some kind of extravagance. On the contrary, this was taken as demonstrating their understanding of the value in good quality. As one shopper noted with at least a hint of disdain at my own appearance, such goods are really money savers because they are 'ever so much better' and last 'ever so much longer' than the kind of low-quality merchandise which I clearly patronized. The point emerged in one case through a comparison made by a wife who came from a relatively wealthy family with her husband whose background was quite impoverished:

A I like to buy real quality. Whereas if I am shopping for food, I am looking always to get the best bargain. I look after the pennies but Dennis would rather look after the pounds. For me buying cheap furniture is in a way an extravagance, because it's going to fall to pieces. And that's all to do with your outlook on life. You know me, never having had any problem about money, I don't find, I would rather buy something that was more expensive, while they never had anything so they would make do.

Clearly then, the particular strategies of thrift are based on factors related to the wider identity of individual and household in terms of class, reputation and many other attributes. But it does not follow that these contextual factors in any way lessen the sense that they are simultaneously all equally effective means by which these people can see themselves as thrifty. However extravagant a household might seem to an outsider, they may understand themselves as experts in the arts of saving money, through the way in which they spend it. For them it may be the poor who are profligate because the latter don't understand how to spend 'properly'. They themselves really 'need' a second car or second holiday in order to work more efficiently and thereby save time and money in the long term, while the unemployed don't really 'need' that pint in the local[23] or variety in their diet. There is then no correlation between the saving of money and the sense of thrift.

One of my more standardized questions to most shoppers concerned the idea of shopping as a skill. The response was almost always in terms of thrift. This was often extended to refer not only to the ability to find things at a cheaper price, but also to only buying things one really needed or could afford. Sarah is an impressive example of these values. Her shopping is dominated by buying what are often highly expensive pieces of sports equipment for her son, who is a junior sports champion. To do this, she uses her knowledge as a market trader to bring exceptional skills to her work as a consumer, finding substitutes for expensive items or genuine bargain outlets, but also never buying things she doesn't see herself as strictly needing. She is, however, almost unique within the street in this regard. For most people saving is a way of spending.

Where spending is the dominant form of saving this is likely to result in ambivalence about materialism. In the case of one couple, both the husband and wife are quite obsessive about saving money, notwithstanding that they represented one of the better-off households in the area. But their strategies were entirely opposed. For the wife, sales were her major form of spending and this was something she enjoyed. She was quite clear about hunting out the specials in supermarkets. Her annoyance was very evident when we passed a children's shoe shop with a sale on but where she could not find anything to fit her children. She knew and used a wide range of strategies such as car boot sales and *Loot* to explore the possibilities for further savings. She also had a complex strategy for buying her children second-hand clothing. She is, however, aware that this is not necessarily leading to her spending less overall.

A Certainly the kids have got far more clothes now than they ever would have if I were buying them new. I'm not quite sure how it pans out in terms of total cost, possibly I spend the same sort of money had I got my children new stuff. So in terms of sheer financial balancing out I'm not sure that it is has been that much of a . . .

Her husband is equally concerned with thrift, but in his case this means refusing to buy things rather than buying more things. Indeed, for the last expensive item they purchased, a hi-fi system, he claims to have tried twenty-eight outlets before choosing the cheapest. He constantly referred back to the poverty of his own childhood in Continental Europe and how he could not bring himself to pay the prices asked. But what clearly frustrated him was that his wife from his point of view managed to be inordinately extravagant through applying the same obsessive concern with thrift that he had. This meant he found it very difficult to be as critical of her as he would have liked.

Many shoppers develop similar contradictions when they are considering their use of Tom's, the cheap greengrocer. They know that much of the fruit and vegetables is of such poor quality that they will have to throw it away, but they simply can't resist the sense of a saving they gain by seeing such large quantities of food for their money and they often come out of Tom's with whole trays of half-rotten fruit. There are many versions of this spending more by saving as in the following three examples:

Q Why do you buy cheaper clothes?
A Because I like buying clothes, and I can't keep going out and buying expensive ones! Sometimes most of the clothes that I've got that were more expensive I like very much, and last longer, but somehow the logic still doesn't quite sink through. You'll still get tempted by the odd bargain that probably really isn't a bargain.

Or:

A Oh yes I am, I'm a terrible shopper for that, that's why I fill up trolleys, it's probably why we don't go very often as well. Yeah I'm very influenced by savings especially the ones that they do in Safeways – if you buy one thing you can have something else free or for half price.
Q Do you do a lot of that?
A Yes and I realize I'm doing it, and it's just a mug's game really because we wouldn't have dreamed of buying the other thing anyway but since it's there.

Or:

A I have great fun going in these 50p or a pound shops and buying very tasteful little numbers like this for my friends.
Q Scouring-pad holder?
A Yes well every house should have one, you can't live without one of those can you?
Q Ceramic cow?
A Yes, this is one of our little parties we had. My husband has been away and we had a girl's night at my house and we had a lucky dip and people won desirable objects like this which I go round these junky shops and purchase. You buy the most taste-less things possible. But actually, saying that, I do find those junky shops are really good for things like kid's party bags, and that I mean it's dead-cheap, but it's dead rubbish. But then you can go into Toys 'R' Us and buy a packet of dead-rubbish water pistols or something for £2, and you can go in these shops and buy something that isn't quite as awful for about 50p. So I think for that sort of thing, and if the kids have got some spending money they can go and buy some felt tips or something. So I do use those quite a bit but I wouldn't say because I particularly like what they sell it's just that they have a purpose.

As one continues to trawl through the complexities of shopping for bargains, the whole relationship between spending and saving comes into question. Are people buying specials in order to spend more or are they spending more in order to save? What is clear is that the simple relationship of thrift as a means towards an overall saving which is an end does not hold for most shoppers. It is just as reasonable to see thrift as the end in itself, that is people are going shopping in order to have the experience of saving money. For some the thrill is in the bargain and it almost doesn't matter how much one spends in order to achieve it. It is also clear that although the forms of thrift differ considerably across class and income group, thrift itself is as important a factor in shopping for the wealthy as it is for the poor. After all, it is a common cliché on the street that the rich are rich because they are thrifty.

Instead then of trying to understand thrift in terms of budgets, it is perhaps better to consider its place in the very experience of shopping itself. It is abundantly clear that provisioning presents more and more opportunities for shopping to be experienced as a form of saving money. The major exception to this is probably the concept of the treat or leisure shopping, such as on holiday, when the very point of shopping is to be extravagant. In short, at the centre of almost all provisioning today is an experience by which what begins as an act of spending is transformed into an experience of saving. That this should be the central ritual of contemporary shopping will become an important component of the overall theoretical argument of this essay.

The Exception

Before concluding the ethnographic representation of shopping with a description of the discourse of shopping, it seems the appropriate time to introduce you to Mary. Mary is the person, whom I suspect by now many of you have all been waiting to meet – in some cases longing to meet. Mary probably couldn't care less about any of what she would probably see as the sanctimonious crap I have been writing about so far. Mary is also a single mother living on the council estate, but Mary has what is currently called 'attitude'. Even on first encounter it was evident that Mary had an aura of sexuality about her, quite a rare attribute in this particular street.

Although Mary's parents had migrated to Britain from Central Europe she had lost any evident trace of these origins. Mary's children were extremely well behaved, and are required to undertake a good deal of the labour of household cleaning. They are also, in the form of child benefit, an important element in her income. I saw no evidence that Mary was neglectful as a parent, and for all I know it may well be that her children benefited from the relative lack of the complex projections of guilt and anxiety that is the concomitant of love in many households. She was engaged in some studying but was also managing to have a very good time on the limited money she had available. Much of this was based on a series of sexual relationships. When actually buying goods, Mary was primarily directed at containing the pragmatics of provisioning into the smallest possible space and thereby opening up as much time and money as she could for enjoying herself. But given this pragmatism, her shopping was also as hedonistic and materialistic as she could make it. Her major interest seemed to be the store detective who had already made several passes at her.

The following is an extract from a general conversation within which we were discussing the idea of shopping as a skill.

A They're [her children] not learning from me very well because I'm not a good example! They need to learn it from my grand-mother who really does shop wisely and only buys exactly what she needs and only buys like bargain brands and don't ever, won't ever, buy anything just for the fun of it. I'm not a good example, I go shopping too much. I probably buy too much and yes I think I haven't really mastered that skill really.
Q Do you see thrift as a skill?
A I think that if you're a clever shopper you'd only ever buy what you want. If you're buying an outfit you'd only buy an outfit that will go with thousands of other outfits and that kind of thing. Well I don't do that. If I see something I might buy it and then when I get home think I'm glad I got that because it might go with that. In that sense I'm not very good . . .
. . .
A Well it was my birthday so I had some birthday money. So I bought things that maybe I wouldn't think about. Like I bought some sunglasses that I did need but I probably wouldn't have bought such expensive ones. They weren't that expensive but I bought them without thinking, in fact, that whole day I didn't look at prices at all, which is really nice. I could live like that. So I bought myself some sunglasses, I think that were a bit over the top but then I did have a reason because it was my birthday.
Q Would you say you were thrifty?
A No I'm not really no, it may look like I am, but I blow, I do spend money on things that I don't need. Like the other day I went and bought myself two pairs of shoes or something or if I'm depressed I spend money so.
Q When depressed what do you buy?

A What do I do. I buy perfume or something for my hair or just real kind of luxury things, really I might go and buy myself a top that I don't really need, silly things or underwear you know.
Q Do you see it as a treat?
A No I don't think, it's a, I just think it's something, it's almost because, you know you haven't really got the money. It only gets you back at the end because you'll suffer in the end but, or I'll go out and say that I'm going to spend some money tonight and I'll go out somewhere that I shouldn't that's more expensive.
Q You mean to...
A To a nightclub or something, or out for dinner or something like that.
Q Are you living on child benefit?
A And my grant which is non-existent really... Last year I was just very poor, but I didn't work because I'd rather be poor and spend time going to the park than...

What this discussion suggests is that, even as a negative case, Mary expressed an important consistency in relation to the topics and the values so far discussed. Mary has no particular interest in sales, and while she understands why thrift is admired as a skill, she simply does not desire to be that kind of person. She clearly has treats, as during her birthday, but in this case she aspires to make all her shopping as treat-like as she can get away with, so the treat becomes the apotheosis rather than the exception. Mary certainly has a keen interest in shopping for love in supermarkets, but in her case the love interest is primarily that of sex. Mary was not a typical informant, but as the next section demonstrates she is a crucial point of reference for all my informants.

There are other shoppers who seem to be like Mary, some even more hedonistically driven, but I have chosen Mary because she is a low-income mother. My expectation was that this would have been the attitude largely of teenagers or young professional singles, that conform to the concept of yuppies. In practice I saw too few teenagers, and the young professional singles seemed mainly obsessed with establishing long-term stable relationships that they didn't presently have. The best example of hedonism apart from Mary lived within a relatively wealthy stable nuclear family. The point, however, of emphasizing Mary is simply that hedonism did not prove to be socially situated where it might have been predicted, though any conclusion would have to be highly tentative since there were simply not enough examples of hedonistic shoppers during this study to feel comfortable in generalizing about this behaviour. The dominant ethos throughout the class levels was one of respectability and thrift.

Mary is also instructive in that she works to make the act of shopping conform as far as possible to other aspects of her identity and interests. This raises the problem involved in isolating shopping as a topic of investigation. There are shoppers who conform well to the ideals of thrift and shopping skill, where these are quite consistent with many other aspects of their identity, for example, respectability or conscientiousness. There are others, however, who might be more like Mary with respect to other domains of life such as the transience of their relationships but who, unlike her, use shopping to conform to the dominant ideal of devotional practice. The implication is that shopping has its own integrity and has become a means for objectifying certain values. This is a primary conclusion of this essay. This need not imply a homogeneity of shoppers. Some aspects of shopping such as the discourse about to be discussed are entirely homogenous; others which are not the topic of this particular essay are much more diverse. Similarly, some shoppers find that the values manifested through shopping conform to the values they express in many other domains, while for others different practices are used to explore and express quite diverse aspects of their identity.[24]

The Discourse of Shopping

It might be thought that after all this emphasis upon ethnographic observation, I would be claiming that my approach is one that is respectful of my informants' own views and perspectives. I might be expected to attack a whole series of more abstract writers, perhaps in sociology or cultural studies,[25] who have written on shopping without having engaged in long-term observation of shopping. I might have claimed that once one talks to the people involved, as on this street, love (as a theme) comes shining through. I do not make any of these claims. Quite apart from the simplistic positivism that would be involved, based around a false aura that is supposed to surround ethnography that is 'true' to and respectful of the informant, any such claim could be quickly and easily refuted.

On the contrary, I would suggest that the theories I oppose, those based on the idea that shopping is largely centred upon hedonism and materialism, are actually much closer to the shoppers' own views and more respectful of my own informants' perspectives than is the theory I will develop here. My own theoretical stance can only be sustained by a refusal, of almost Lévi-Straussian proportions, to acknowledge and be drawn by my informants. Any academic who works within the contemporary ethnographic fashion of 'listening' with sensitivity to informants, and then representing them directly rather than imposing an authoritarian analysis upon their voices and actions, must undoubtedly eschew all that I will have to say about the nature of provisioning and fall back behind the ranks of conventional theories of shopping. This becomes evident as soon as we turn from an observational perspective on shopping to the alternative perspective of recording informants' own accounts and explanations of shopping – the discourse of shopping.

By discourse I mean nothing more pretentious than that which people tend to say about shopping as a general topic. The implication of this term is quite distinct from that of ideology. The latter term has been employed to direct us to what is not said, but is implicit in practices and might well be denied in an interview context. Discourse is used here in a literal sense to refer to what people first say about a topic without any prompting or delving. Most of the extracts from conversations that have been presented in the previous sections of this chapter were extracted from detailed discussions of particular shopping acts, such as why a particular product was purchased, or the skills involved in shopping. In these conversations people did not see themselves as trying to account for shopping more generally, but rather were concerned with the detailed technologies and moralities of provisioning. Even more of the evidence comes from the experience of accompanied shopping and careful observation devoted to what shoppers actually do as against their representations of this practice. The situation is very different if one asks these same people about shopping in general.

The idea that there exists a discourse, as opposed to its plural 'discourses', of shopping suggests either an astonishing degree of generalization on my part or on the part of those studied. As noted at the outset of this essay, this street is extremely diverse. It is highly differentiated by class, and both my figures and those of the local primary school suggest that this area includes one of the greatest diversities of cultural backgrounds anywhere in Britain. This poses a problem for anthropological analysis. The use of the term 'culture' in that discipline has tended to imply something deep, a system of values and symbolic logics with a long trajectory behind them. Culture has become a sign of authenticity that implies that when people come together from different origins those backgrounds should remain of considerable importance as agents of continued differentiation and, in a sense, conservatism. This implies that one should not be able to use any similar term to that of 'culture' for the non-community which I was studying.

While there are topics within this research for which this expected implication of culture held when recast as ethnicity,[26] there were others where it was entirely repudiated. The finding that there is only a single discourse about shopping would be an exemplary case of the fallibility of an assumption that culture acts as a conservative habitus limiting new conceptualizations. Since starting on this research project I have told some hundreds of people that I am studying shopping, most commonly in response to that perennial opening line 'and what do you do?' I have been struck by the extraordinary uniformity of the response to my declared interest. This does not seem to vary by class, by education or by regional background or origin. It is as characteristic of the many other anthropologists I have spoken to as it is of working-class housewives on the street. The response takes several forms but the most common is as follows: 'Oh, if you are studying shopping, the person you really should meet is my aunt/grandmother/cousin etc. She is a real shopper, a veritable shopaholic.' Another version is: 'Well if you are interested in shopping you really must visit Lakeside/West Edmonton/the Mall of America/the Metro Centre – that place is just too much.' Associated with this may be the statement that 'I just adore shopping, it's my greatest pleasure in life' or an equally strong 'I loathe shopping, if you want to know about shopping talk to my partner she/he has got a degree in shopping.'

There are many variations to these responses but a single perspective links them all. When I tell people that I am studying shopping this proposal never[27] evokes the experience of shopping that I actually studied, which is the kind of shopping that most people actually do. It is as though provisioning is not in fact shopping. The shopping that is evoked by the abstract term 'shopping' as a topic to be studied, which people immediately suppose I must be studying, or ought to be studying, is always an extreme form of shopping, an over-the-top activity devoted largely to indulging itself. The core connotations of this act are firstly materialism – that is an obsessional desire to buy things *per se* and secondly hedonism – that is a highly self-indulgent form of pleasure and leisure. Shopping here is primarily an act of spending, preferably spending large amounts of money, almost without a care for the consequences. Ideally, this will take place in some mall which abstracts shopping from all other contexts and becomes a framed environment solely devoted to this abstract pursuit of shopping for its own sake. In considering the general discourse of shopping, my final example of Mary moves from being the exception, to the nearest person in my study to approximate to a 'true' shopper.

The ethnographic study was carried out as part of a larger project involving both anthropologists and geographers. One of the reasons for this interdisciplinarity is that it allowed for a plurality of research techniques. In particular, there was a gradation from a questionnaire administered at the shopping centres, through focus groups to ethnography.[28] The ideal of shopping as pleasure and leisure follows this same gradation. It is most conspicuous at the level of the questionnaire. This reflects many journalistic stories (which may be apocryphal but represent widely held beliefs) about surveys of women that show that their greatest source of pleasure is shopping, and that this scores over and above sex, their children and other potential rivals. The results of our own questionnaire were not so extreme, but pleasure and leisure play a prominent role in the answers given. Turning from questionnaires to focus groups, the stress on pleasure and leisure is more variable, depending upon the nature of the particular group. Mothers with small children, for example, were more likely to focus upon the trials and tribulations of shopping, while youths place more of an emphasis upon hedonistic browsing. Taken as a whole, however, leisure and pleasure are still a significant element within the focus group discussions, though they are not as prominent here as in questionnaire responses.

When one comes to the ethnography, the same story can be told during interviews where shopping was discussed in the abstract; but where ethnography becomes participant observation the situation is entirely different. The idea of shopping as pleasure is closely associated with the idea of shopping as leisure. Campbell (forthcoming) provides one explanation for this close association. He argues that shopping under the constraint of necessity is likely to be viewed as work, while the unconstrained freedom to browse and choose is experienced as a relatively free expression of agency. For this reason, shopping as pleasure is often associated with holiday times, as something to do when free from other burdens, or the need for particular items. But in the context of the street ethnography, this pleasure of shopping was virtually non-existent, because the category of leisure was itself largely absent during the day. Despite enormous variations in their circumstances, almost all householders saw themselves, on a day-to-day basis, as extremely busy. They understood themselves as never having enough time to do the things they felt they needed to do. The ideal of shopping as leisure could not be realized, because in the event shopping was always carried out under the constraints of competition for the time spent in shopping. In the case of housewives in part-time work this is hardly surprising, but even the single elderly tended to present themselves as always busy, never really having time.[29] Many carried in their heads relatively organized schedules for themselves that, whether real or not, managed to act to convince their authors that their time was still as important, and as much in need of husbanding, as that of those in work and with clear commitments. It is possible that the situation would be very different in, for example, a village setting (though I doubt this). At any rate the ethnography suggested that to live in North London is to be busy, almost irrespective of the use of time. As such, a conceptualization of shopping that depends upon its relationship to leisure is hardly ever realized in everyday life.[30]

Faced with such uniformity in people's responses to the idea that I am studying shopping, I will use this information later on to draw a conclusion at the same level of generalization as that to be found in conventional anthropological analyses where applied to small-scale and homogeneous communities. This raises two connected questions. How is this uniformity compatible with the extraordinary diversity in background and social position of the people who present this stock response, and why should there exist such a massive disparity between a discourse provoked by any discussion of shopping in general and the experience of shopping as an activity? With regard to the first issue, it may be best to accept that while some elements of normative practice will meet resistances to conformity based on either habitus or the desire to remain different, in other cases conventional opinions are quickly learnt. It may take no more time for immigrants into British society to pick up what are the legitimate things to say and think about shopping as an abstraction than it does to learn how to negotiate a supermarket.

This is undoubtedly facilitated by the centrality of this discourse of shopping to what can be called the journalistic mode. I will not trouble to give examples of the journalistic representation of shopping as an extravagant bout of hedonism and materialism since I am confident that readers will find examples quickly enough from their own newspapers and media accounts.[31] It is ubiquitous. It is also hallowed in popular culture images. Although the most overt sexism of older cartoon strips such as Blondie and the Gambols with their portrayal of mindless shopping by gullible wives is somewhat tempered, the contemporary examples are only slightly more nuanced. Today a strip cartoon is more likely to present the mindless shopper dazzled by the possibilities of virtual reality shopping or the shoppers' TV channel (e.g. Doonesbury), but the genre has changed little. Journalists are also more likely to dwell upon the wonders of commerce as a machine for selling goods, for example, the kinds of data available to supermarkets through store cards, that allow them to predict shoppers' behaviour. This means that the image of the insatiable shopper is complemented by the portrayal of the shopper as victim, unable to escape from the entrapments of capitalist technology.[32] Nevertheless, the effect in terms of the representation of shopping in general is much the same. In both cases shoppers are assumed to act as 'true' shoppers in the sense given by this discourse of shopping.

The ubiquity of discussion about shopping as extravagance and 'mindless' hedonistic materialism plays a major role in the more dominant ideologies of our time.[33] There exists a general assumption that people who possess more goods must be more materialistic than people without. It does not matter that an anthropologist working in the Amazonian forest can tell how he was exasperated by the degree to which these relatively possession-free Amerindians exhibited a greed and acquisitiveness that he had never before encountered. Or that even American anthropologists stand aghast at the high level of consumerism amongst lowland South American Indians (Hugh-Jones 1992). At the level of discourse, all such forest dwellers must be equated with Sahlins (1972) 'original affluent society', that is a society without desire. Meanwhile the occidentalist myth (Carrier 1995b) portrays ourselves as a society with unlimited desire as part of this opposition between the authenticity of noble savages and the inauthentic superficiality of ourselves.

I have argued elsewhere that it makes little sense to assume that the desires behind consumption commonly found within, for example, Norway, have necessarily much in common with those to be found in the United States (Miller 1995: 27–8), but to question the myth of materialism and hedonistic greed as a character of the first-world consumer is to threaten a primary attribute in the self-characterization of modern identity. The people of this street conform well to these contradictions. For them also, the activity in which they engaged on an almost daily basis made no impression whatsoever upon their conformity to a discourse about shopping that rested upon a fantastic vision which most of them rarely, if ever, realized. The answers to these two questions are therefore closely connected. It is the degree of abstraction of this discourse away from practice and experience that makes it so quickly and easily assimilated amongst people from a wide variety of backgrounds. This allows it to become a normative and immediate response elicited by questions about shopping in general. At this abstract level of discourse the social and cultural backgrounds of the speaker have become entirely irrelevant.

There remains, however, the basic discrepancy between discourse and practice to be accounted for. That which is made explicit in discourse is clearly quite contrary to the ideologies which remain implicit in practice. This will turn out to be critical to an understanding of the cosmological foundation of shopping. But for the present a consideration of the abstract discourse of shopping completes an extraction of 'jigsaw' pieces from the ethnographic encounter. In ending with the dissonance between practice and discourse it should be clear that at least at this point these pieces will not easily fit together to make a clear portrait. The alignment of love, the treat and thrift is disrupted by a simultaneously held representation of shopping that refers to none of them. Joining them to form a coherent and focused image will only be accomplished through the use of theory. This theory will now be extracted from the study of what at first will appear to be the quite irrelevant phenomenon of sacrificial ritual.

2
Shopping as Sacrifice

In turning to the topic of sacrifice, the approach taken will be to investigate theories of an underlying structure to these types of ritual. The first section will briefly consider the nature of sacrifice and the variety of theories and approaches that has been applied to this topic, ending with a discussion of Bataille, who most clearly equated the underlying logic of sacrifice with that of consumption. The categories extracted from the ethnography of shopping will then be applied to the structure that has been generalized through the literature on sacrifice to create a theory of shopping as sacrifice. At first this exercise stands in its own right, but in chapter 3 the implications of this juxtaposition will be considered more carefully through an examination of other subjects and objects of devotion.

Two principal arguments will be made for a relationship between sacrifice and shopping. The first will be based on the observation that both cases represent a key moment when the labour of production is turned into the process of consumption. In both cases the fear is expressed of mere mundane or materialistic consumption and the rituals are designed to ensure that goods are first used for reaffirming transcendent goals. The second link is at the level of structure. It will be argued that there is a clear analogy between the main stages of sacrifice and shopping as devotional rites. At the same time the chapter will serve as a rejection of the currently most popular argument for a link between sacrifice and shopping, an argument based on a theory of violence.

Sacrifice

The discussion of sacrifice needs to be introduced with a warning. Detienne (1989: 20), after demonstrating how many of the earlier and more general theories of sacrifice seem to have been impelled by a trajectory which led to the Christian sacrifice of the deity as their end point, suggests that any attempt at a general theory of sacrifice is mistaken 'both because it gathers into one artificial type elements taken from here and there in the symbolic fabric of societies and because it reveals the surprising power of annexation that Christianity still subtly exercises on the thought of these historians and sociologists who were convinced they were inventing a new science.' One of the more interesting recent attempts at a theory which uses evidence from sacrifice (Bloch 1992) starts with the premiss that the best equivalent to sacrifice in one society may be what on the surface looks like quite a different ritual practice such as initiation in another society. Finally, it would hardly behove me to attempt any pedantic or tight definition of sacrifice, when my purpose is to apply these ideas to the topic of shopping where (even) I would grant that this is more an act of analogy than one of identity.

So rather than attempting to define sacrifice, I intend merely to note some generalizations which have been made in the literature on sacrifice, while acknowledging that there may also be considerable differences between both the content and the cosmological significance of what went on in biblical sacrifice as against contemporary West Africa (de Heusch 1985), or between Valeri's (1985) careful exposition of sacrifice in Hawaii as against recent considerations of violence in ancient Greece (Burkert 1983, Girard 1977, Hamerton-Kelly 1987). In chapter 3 a rather more dia-chronic approach is taken to sacrifice which links the legacy of such devotional rites with the development of the ethos of love identified here with shopping.

The analogies are better traced to the implications of the debate that followed Hubert and Mauss's (1964, but originally published in 1898) classic text on sacrifice. This was based mainly on rituals described for ancient India (Vedic religion) and biblical sources. There are two main points I want to take from Hubert and Mauss. The first is their structuralism, by which is meant their sense that the act of sacrifice needs to be analytically dis-sected into its various moments, but that to be properly under-stood one has then to set these various elements, or stages of which the sacrifice is composed, back within a perspective upon sacrifice as a whole. Equally valuable is their observation that sacrifice is ultimately about constituting a relationship between those involved and a transcendent or sacred world. Sacrifice opens up this relationship, and irrespective of whether one wishes to call this a communication or an exchange, its effect is to create the conditions for association and thereby a flow of efficacy. This emphasis upon entering into a relationship with the deity is also central to a tradition of analysis which harks back to Robertson Smith (Beidelman 1974: 53, Robertson Smith 1894). But taken from a materialist or sceptical perspective, this might also be viewed as a primary means by which humanity constitutes and reproduces its sense of the transcendent. By purporting to be in relation to the divine we most efficiently give testament to its existence, to the object of our devotion. Sacrifice therefore can be held to constitute objects of devotion as well as communicate with them.[34]

To elaborate on the first point, Hubert and Mauss, by dividing the sacrifice into its component elements, are able to consider the possibilities latent in each of these, before they are subsumed by the whole. They stress that a sacrifice differs from the mere con-secration of an object, in that during sacrifice the object is actually destroyed or consumed. It is this act of expenditure or destruction that gives sacrifice its additional potency (1964: 12). Later authors have argued that this stage of destructive consumption seems to unleash images of violence that are the crux of sacrifice. But Hubert and Mauss, rather than dwelling upon this act of destruction in and of itself, prefer to concentrate on its place within a process. Sacrifice proceeds through various stages which result in a series of transformations, not only in the victim, but more especially in the sacrifier, that is the person or persons to whom the benefits of the sacrifice will accrue.

Placed within an overall sequence of increasing followed by decreasing sanctification, the destructive element of expenditure is tamed by its incorporation into sacrifice as a whole. For Hubert and Mauss there are two opposing processes involved. One leads to an accumulation in sacralization and the other moves from the sacred back down to the profane. According to their model the last stages of sacrifice will often be devoted to a kind of cooling down or dissipation of the sacred forces that have been unleashed by the sacrificial contact. The ritual returns, sometimes by stages, from the sacred act of consumption by the divine force down to the eating of the remains of the sacrifice by a human group. Many of the technical details that surround sacrifice are concerned with regulating these stages of transformation, for example, the various rites of sacralization that must be passed through in order for the sacrificer (the person conducting the sacrifice) and the victim to be ready and appropriate for entering into a relationship with the divine. An important rite is often the separation of the victim into that which is burnt and rises up as the sweet-smelling smoke to become the food of the gods and that which is retained and eaten by priests, sacrifier or others.

The next point made by Hubert and Mauss is that the aims of sacrifice may be extremely various. Many sacrifices are based on relatively minor requirements for efficacy such as curing sickness or fulfilling a vow. Many others are fixed sacrifices which are dictated by seasonal festivals or life-cycle events such as birth and marriage. The range of sacrifice extends from these mundane rites up to the most general statement of the absolute devotion of a people to its gods. Sacrifice may be a means of distancing oneself from problematic sacralness as well as gaining sacred power. They insist, however, that notwithstanding the diversity of their purpose, sacrifices remain a generic category because they are all based on the same process of creating a relationship to the divine.

Biblical sacrifice as outlined in the early books of law and custom such as Leviticus and Deuteronomy would exemplify this point. What is first evident is the sheer ubiquity of sacrifice. Apart from the narrative of events and the exposition of law, the descriptions of requirements and contents of sacrifice seem to be the main 'filling' that pads out the text. There are endless and repetitive details about the techniques and requirements for various forms of sin offerings, peace offerings, guilt offerings, burnt offerings, meal offerings and so forth. Sacrifice is found to be a highly routine element in the lives of the people. Given the very strict requirements about the unblemished nature of the sacrificial victim and details for how exactly the sacrifice should be carried out, it was most likely a rather intrusive element in people's lives. As with contemporary Jewish religious practice, people must often have been occupied with the technical details of deciding what constitutes a blemish or where to obtain the appropriate forms of kindling, and avoiding all those factors which could lead to a sacrifice being aborted or annulled as incorrectly carried out. Similarly, in reading about African or ancient Greek sacrifice, the impression is that among other things sacrifice is a rather ordinary and regular form of expenditure. This is particularly the case when sacrifice is related to eating. In ancient Greece all killing of animals for meat was ritualized as sacrifice, while most decisions of any importance required a sacrifice as a precondition.

The biblical texts also reveal a clear gradation from these ordinary sacrifices up to the enormously impressive sacrifices that provide a climax to the annual cycle. During the Day of Atonement service Jews still read about the high priest of the temple, trembling lest his zeal should be doubted, as he goes through a series of complex rites of sacrifice that are described in loving detail. The sacrifice by King Solomon of 220,000 oxen and 120,000 sheep at the dedication of the Temple (1 Kings 8:63)[35] suggests the potential of sacrifice as grand spectacle. Most societies that practise sacrifice seem to have had similar major public rituals of considerable power and sanctity. In these latter cases the acts do not point downwards to the mundanity of the meal but become key moments of religiosity involving massive expenditures. They are moments when one expects a people to have been highly focused upon the awe and majesty of the deity. As a means of constantly reiterating the sense of devotion to the deity it is likely that the sheer ubiquity and routine of minor sacrifice was as efficacious as the grand rituals. This may have been in some measure because they constantly remind the sacrifier of the awe and power of those occasions that become in their grandeur the quintessence of sacrificial relationships to the divinity.

It may well be the rather practical use of sacrifice in securing a range of ordinary requests and needs that is one of the most important means by which divinity is itself affirmed, that is by which people have a sense of the transcendent. As Hubert and Mauss note, 'the act of abnegation implicit in every sacrifice, by recalling frequently to the consciousness of the individual the presence of collective forces, in fact sustains their ideal existence' (1964: 102), i.e. the deity is thereby renewed in its spiritual character. This point would hold even if sacrifice does not necessarily involve abnegation, a point made for African sacrifice (de Heusch 1985).

Hubert and Mauss provide us with a perspective on sacrifice that understands this act as a totalizing ritual. Sacrifice is held to transform what might otherwise have been merely acts of expenditure or consumption, and turn them into a primary means by which the transcendent is affirmed. The true act of sacrifice seems to be one that is directed as a devotional act to a divine agent. We may talk of sacrifice for the sake of society, as in the sacrifice of persons in war, or the self-sacrifice of the housewife to her household. When we do so, the term takes on the sense of metaphor or analogy as against the ritual and routinized acts of sacrifice that constitute, through constant re-recognition, the divine itself. To make an analogy with shopping I would therefore have to demonstrate that shopping is a regular act that turns expenditure into a devotional ritual that constantly reaffirms some transcendent force, and thereby becomes a primary means by which the transcendent is constituted.

The approach to sacrifice developed by Hubert and Mauss has been both refined and challenged subsequently by many others. Luc de Heusch (1985) provides one of the most sustained critiques of their model and its later application by Evans-Pritchard, attacking the over-emphasis upon both Vedic and Judeo-Christian traditions. He also denies the universalism of the basic links they forge around an opposition between the sacred and the profane. The relativism introduced by a comparative perspective based on Africa demonstrates that there are bound to be exceptions to any such modelling. For example, there are societies for whom domestic sacrifice is clearly a separate sphere from any core cosmological sacrifice that tends to re-enact the birth of the universe (ibid.: 215). In turn, de Heusch introduces through the African material a number of themes that may not appear so strongly elsewhere. But at the same time he argues that there remains merit in a comparative study of sacrifice, and in many ways he refines rather than repudiates the work of seeing sacrifice as a series of stages tending to revolve around common themes.

If the argument of this essay tends to follow Hubert and Mauss in their generalities rather than those that emerge from a comparative analysis of African sacrifice, it is in part a suspicion that the Judeo-Christian traditions, and their duality of the sacred and profane may maintain some continuity with a study of shopping that is based in North London – a possibility that will be explored further in chapter 3. The theory developed here does not depend upon their's being a universal model, or the absence of alternative universal models. Once the general structure is established, it is possible to develop the theory to a next stage. This involves following the subsequent literature which tends to focus on individual elements within the sacrifice, suggesting that in certain times and places some particular aspect had become the focus of the ritual as a whole. A part of the overall sequence that is a merely minor part of sacrifice in one society is found to be the dominant feature for another.

The recent debates on sacrifice in ancient Greece exemplify this trend particularly well. Here as elsewhere a focus on violence has become quite fashionable in recent works (Burkert 1983, Girard 1977, Hamerton-Kelly 1987), a theme that will be returned to below. This literature creates an intense focus upon a single act within the sacrifice, that is the act of killing. It serves to abstract this from the sacrifice as a whole in order to consider its implications. Another common theme is of sacrifice as referring back to the original creation of the world and in particular the classification of humanity within it. This is an important feature in ancient Vedic sacrifice and some contemporary African sacrifice where the emphasis is on the renewal of social and individual order (de Heusch 1985: 192–202). While this theme might be absent in some sacrificial traditions it is common to many, probably rather more common than the elaboration or expiation of violence.

If the new writings about violence focus upon one end of the ritual, then Detienne and Vernant (1989) represent another approach focusing upon a later stage of sacrifice and again applying this to the material from ancient Greece. Their concern is with the communal meal which follows the sacrifice and the distribution of the portions of the animal. The various papers in their book examine different aspects of this meal, but taken together they demonstrate the crucial importance of the subsequent distribution of the animal's parts as a means of objectifying the social relations of the community.[36] Although there is reference to a more egalitarian distribution in the Homeric period, the primary concern of their book is the later period with its manifestation and sanctification of difference both in terms of social hierarchy and in the classification of certain groups such as women or priests. Often sacrifice served not only to represent these classifications but, as in ancient Judaism, provided a significant contribution to the priestly caste, for whom 'a good part of the revenue needed to support the priesthood accrued in the form of sacrifices' (Levine 1989: xiii).

Clear parallels may also be drawn between the arguments being put forward by Detienne and a standard rite of contemporary Hinduism. In Hinduism almost any ritual occasion that involves a visit to the temple and the making of an offering involves the distribution of *prasad*.[37] This is understood to be the leftovers of the offering given to the deity which are then to be consumed by humanity. Often these are standard forms such as round white sweets, or bags of sweet flour with nuts and raisins. They are either distributed amongst those engaged in the ritual or taken and given to a much wider body of people in the area. They are symbolically linked to another concept called *jutha*, which is the pollution incurred when people eat meals. This includes the pollution of the utensils, the food or anything which might have been in contact with saliva. *Jutha* clearly marks hierarchy in that such polluted leftovers are only suitable for consumption by inferior castes and even the cleaning of the utensils should be by someone of inferior status to the eater. The implication of *prasad* then is that human beings by agreeing to eat the leftovers of the gods demonstrate their own inferiority to the gods. As Parry puts it, 'Just as the *jutha* of the high castes is pure enough to be consumed by the lower castes, so the sacramental *prasad*, the food which is consecrated to the deities and is distributed after every *puja* [act of worship] to all the worshippers, is technically divine *jutha*, (Parry 1979: 100). The point being made by Detienne with respect to the distribution of sacrificial foods is therefore even clearer in Hinduism. There is an extensive literature, especially following Dumont (1970) and Marriot (1968), that has emphasized the importance of commensality in both the eating and the transaction of foods as fundamental to the objectification and sustaining of social difference and especially caste hierarchy in Hindu society.

The recent literature on sacrifice draws attention to particular stages within the rites and their consequences. But to retain the advances made by Hubert and Mauss means remembering that an over-emphasis on one such stage can lead to a neglect of other stages. For example, Bloch suggests that the emphasis upon the communal meal by Detienne leads to a neglect of issues to do with the self-identification of the sacrifier with the victim (Bloch 1992: 30). One of the reasons for recalling the latter is that it may well play a role in the subsequent importance of sacrifice as a key metaphor in secular society developed through the use of the term 'self-sacrifice'.

There is one final aspect of sacrifice which needs to be addressed and which brings us back to the issue of sacrifice as a whole. This is hinted at, but never fully explored in the comparative

literature, and consists of the relationship of sacrifice to consumption. Sacrifice is always an act of consumption, a form of
expenditure through which something or someone is consumed.
The presence of sacrifice in consumption varies. In some cases all
eating of meat depends on prior sacrificial rites. In other societies
the sheer mundane nature of sacrifice, the number of different
activities that required it, also suggests that sacrifice accounted
for a rather major element of the spending of what has been
produced. Where this was not the case with respect to quantity
it may well have been true for quality, in that the very best
animals and foodstuffs are offered to the gods. In many places
also it is the moment of movement from production to consumption which is symbolized in the sacrifice of the first-fruits or first-
born. It is noticeable that it is the harvest festival of Sukkot
which seems to represent the peak of the sacrificial calendar of
ancient Judaism at least in terms of the sheer abundance of sacrifices performed (Milgrom 1989: 247–50).

There is a symbolic as well as a substantive connection between sacrifice and mundane consumption in many cases, as found
in the representational aspects of the meal. In ancient Judaism
there are many clear parallels and also oppositions between sacrifice and eating meals. At one level sacrifices appear to be themselves meals. Most of the routine calendrical animal sacrifices
have their complement in wheat offerings, libations of wine and
the addition of salt, suggesting the basic ingredients of meals
(Leviticus 2: 13). In some cases the cereal content grows in proportion to that of the meat offered (Milgrom 1991: 198). A basic
category of sacrifice, the *zevah*, may be seen as a shared meal
between priests, worshippers and God (Levine 1989: 16). The
only acceptable animals for sacrifice are the domestic creatures
that are also used for domestic consumption.

After the destruction of the temple in Jerusalem all eating of
meals becomes a form of sacrifice with all consumers as priests,
this being symbolized by the appropriation of sacrificial rites for
all meals such as the washing of hands and the sprinkling of salt
(Milgrom 1983: 141). On the other hand there is a clear division
between the two in that the materials used for the sacrifice must

be of a purer unblemished form compared to those used for ordinary meals. While most of the meat may be eaten by humans, there are other sections of the animal, including the blood, which are sacred as the life-force and therefore must be rendered back to the divinity to whom alone life as a quality belongs. These parts are therefore never available for human consumption. This is the case for the consumption of all animals and not just those used in sacrifice (ibid.: 104–7).

In many societies the effect of these various relationships between sacrifice and consumption is to subsume the general sense of expenditure or spending within an economy of devotion. The rites of sacrifice ensured that the most important spending was spending on the gods. There was a route created from spending in general, which had no inherent religiosity, to minor sacrificial acts that spoke to the existence of the divine, through to the great acts of resplendent sacrifice, where everything that was profane was banished in direct communion with the sense of the divine. This gradation placed the whole arena of expenditure within the compass of religious devotion in making consumption the crucial intermediary by which the divine was constituted and related to.

To conclude: the defining feature of sacrifice is that moment in which the object of sacrifice is literally consumed. Most commonly it is livestock or plants that have been up to that point the focus of labour and production. The act of sacrifice then takes the moment at which production is transmuted into consumption and appropriates it for the purpose of sanctification and receiving the powers of transcendent objects of devotion on behalf of individuals and society. Sacrifice ensures that the very best of what society has produced is effectively and efficiently spent to obtain not merely mundane provisioning but the benefits of a relationship of love and devotion to a divine force. This is achieved through some awe-inspiring acts of public sacrifice, but in most sacrificial cultures it is also suffused within practices of sacrifice that are a constant feature of life. That which is experienced as a quite practical and mundane relationship between a people and a transcendent being is constantly reconstituted and affirmed through sacrifice.

▨▨ The Contribution of Bataille ▨▨

Although the general anthropological literature on sacrifice does not dwell upon the relationship between sacrifice as consumption and spending more generally, my argument does have one very obvious precedent in the work of the French philosopher Georges Bataille. Although my conclusions will in many respects be, not just opposed, but systematically opposed, to those of Bataille, we share a number of key premises, of which the most important is the equating of sacrifice with consumption. The debt must therefore be acknowledged. This same equation was central to Bataille's thinking.

The clearest exposition of his argument comes in one of Bataille's most important works *La Part Maudite*, published in 1949, the first volume of which has been translated as *The Accursed Share* (Bataille 1988). Bataille stresses that this is a work on the general political economy, but unlike most such studies which focus upon production his work is focused upon consumption. In as far as I understand it the argument runs as follows. The initial premiss is, to say the least, rather strange: it is the idea that the world receives excess energy (initially from the sun) that must be got rid of – 'it is not necessity but its contrary "luxury" that presents living matter and mankind with their fundamental problems' (ibid.: 12) This is the problem of excess. Fortunately this opening section is misleading, since as one reads on further one finds that the larger reasoning behind Bataille's project, and that from which its passion is derived, has nothing much to do with energy *per se*, but is rather a critique of the culture and society of his time.

Like many of his contemporaries (and our contemporaries) Bataille uses his earlier exposure to the writings of Hegel and Marx to argue that capitalist society is one in which we are reduced to mere utility and the problematics of commodities as things.

> Once the world of things was posited, man himself became one of the things of this world, at least for the time in which he laboured. It is this degradation that man has always tried to escape. In his strange myths, in his cruel rites, man is in search of a lost intimacy

from the first. Religion is this long effort and this anguished quest: it is always a matter of detaching from the real order, from the poverty of things, and of restoring the divine order. (ibid.: 57)

Bataille's constant enemy is the utilitarian, a world reduced to interest and pragmatism. For Bataille the end of formal religion should have been the liberation of the true religious impulse, that is of the ability of human kind to have a higher grounding in the world. This pure religion would be unsullied by the institutionalized religions that had existed up to that time. Instead, Bataille argues that Nietzsche's death of God, the moment of potential liberation, has become merely the moment of complete surrender to a logic of commodities. He takes his culprit from the work of Weber on the link between Protestantism and especially Calvinism and capitalism. For Bataille, Calvinism drew the world down towards mere utility and the complete abandonment of sanctity, leading to the relegation of mankind to gloryless activity. This process is then continued in different versions both within capitalism and Marxism, although the latter exhibits for Bataille many more interesting and nuanced contradictions and ambivalences about utility than the former.

Bataille asserts (I believe correctly) the centrality of consumption to capitalism and the contemporary world. What he requires therefore is an image of some alternative form of consumption, a consumption that is not merely the handmaiden to profitability and a subservience to things. He finds this model of consumption in the act of sacrifice, but, not surprisingly, his concept of sacrifice is derived from the requirements of his critique. What fascinates Bataille is the sheer excess of consumption represented by sacrifice, the pure destruction of items that might otherwise have had mere utilitarian value. The best means to restoring what he calls the intimate order is by destroying profitlessly that which might have been used with profit.

His core example is taken from sacrifice amongst the ancient Aztecs (ibid.: 46–61). Bataille draws attention to the value of what is consumed, in this case mainly people. He notes the way the victim is first well treated as an important personage which thereby stresses how much is being, as it were, thrown away in the act of sacrificing these same people. Equally important is the sheer immoderate excess and violence of these acts of consumption. It is this which restores not only our humanity but for Bataille our divinity as against the gross materiality of the calculative. Even better known is Bataille's analysis of the potlatch,[38] derived from the work of Mauss (1966) on the gift. For Bataille, the emphasis should be, not on the accumulation of wealth and power, but on its dissipation in a veritable orgy of destruction. Richman (1982) indicates, through a careful reading of his work, the importance to Bataille of taking from, but also going beyond, Mauss's earlier attempt to see the gift as the negation of the logic of the commodity.

Richman also summarizes a considerable body of literature by Bataille which creates two major analogues for the act of sacrifice – eroticism and violence. For Bataille, many religious practices were likely to have been engaged in this same struggle against utility. He therefore seeks, through a rather old-fashioned genre of anthropology, to extract from various lands and times what he takes to be visions of excess that celebrate a pointlessness and destructive liberation of humanity. Violence is linked to death itself as a sense of complete destructive consumption. As in the Aztec sacrifice, there is often a dwelling upon pain and violence as thereby accomplishing this religious vision. The other analogy is the erotic (Bataille 1987). The erotic does not mean sexuality as part of the creation of relationships and purposeful reproduction, but the sheer excessive expenditure of abstract sexuality committed only to achieving a sense of complete exhaustion as a primary act of consumption and thereby of intimacy in Bataille's religious sense of that term. Many of Bataille's earlier writings concentrate on the erotic vision as an attempt to communicate the possibilities given to our bodies to liberate ourselves through excessive consumption. Eroticism is 'the joy of consuming without return' (Richman 1982: 103). But with the development of more mature work such as *The Accursed Share*, the erotic is reduced to only one such image, along with violence, of the more fundamental conceptualization of the idea of consumption as sacrifice. The consumer's purpose is to annihilate, destroying but also incorporating the objects of desire.

Bataille's writings represent an important working out of one of the many logics of thought that were unleashed with the Enlightenment. In a brilliant essay (1990) on Hegel's understanding of the centrality of acknowledging death in the self-creation of human spirit, Bataille provides a profound and logical explanation of sacrifice as our own vicarious extinction. Since, by definition, we cannot learn from the experience of our own death, we identify with the victim of sacrifice and thus obtain that experience of death which Hegel argues is essential for the development of our humanity. For Bataille, as for Hegel, it is only through consciousness of death that we can come to an appreciation of life.

As an imaginative grounding of dialectical thought, Bataille's essay is fascinating. Unfortunately there is no evidence that this logic, appealing though it might be, has the slightest bearing on actual sacrificial ritual as it has been enacted in the past and present. Despite some attempt to defend Bataille's analysis of sacrifice, Richardson's (1994: 79–85) survey of the evidence concludes along with most commentators that, whether he is writing about Aztec sacrifice or the potlatch, Bataille manages to misunderstand and misrepresent almost every historical and ethnographic source he ever employed. This might be excusable if at least the argument which was derived from these examples had its own merit. But Bataille's attempts to demonstrate the value of transgressive behaviour and, in particular, his explorations of cruelty and pain within eroticism are (I hope) no better guide to the future than they are founded on the past. In practice Bataille demonstrates yet another of those modernist academic pathologies that occur when a particular logic is decontextualized from any social and cultural context as a moment in dialectical thought and followed to its own conclusion with a rather literal representation through enactment.[39]

Although Bataille may have been wrong in his representations of history or ethnography and equally misguided in the conclusions which he drew from them, the vision of excess which Bataille enunciates is a genuine vision that appears and sometimes plagues many of us, at some time or other. The argument developed here is almost the opposite to that of Bataille. Bataille sees the utilitarian as his enemy and feels that it is in transgression that people come to a sense of their humanity. I would argue, by contrast, that under conditions of modernity we constantly fantasize extremes of freedom and constraint, of which Bataille's vision of excess would be an example. But in both capitalist and non-capitalist societies most people come to view their essential humanity in the mechanisms by which these visions are repudiated and resisted through the construction of ethical law. Furthermore, I will argue that, in contrast to Bataille, there is abundant evidence to support my contention.

It would be equally misleading to err in the direction opposite to that of Bataille. The varied, often quite mundane purposes of sacrifice, as portrayed by Hubert and Mauss, could be compared with that of capitalism at a rather superficial level. Many sacrifices could be subject to a calculation that the benefit that will accrue is greater than the resources which will be consumed, and that this is thereby an act from which the sacrifier will profit. But the analogy is false, since unlike capitalism this 'profit' only makes sense as part of a cosmological consideration that generates sacrifice as an act of constitutive devotion. Sacrifice more often involves considerable material loss from profane utility, and its gains are rather through the transmutation of mere material forms into a relationship with higher and transcendent capacities and powers that are associated with the divine. The ultimate benefits are then anything but material.

For the purposes of this essay the important route out of Bataille's analysis lies in his emphasis upon the relationship between consumption and sacrifice. This is much assisted by the development of a more recent academic tradition which has concentrated upon the relationship between violence and sacrifice (Burkert 1983, Girard 1977, Hamerton-Kelly 1987). The emphasis in these writings has been on essentializing violence as a basic human propensity. Sacrifice either expresses violence as inherent in humankind directly or, as in the case of the scapegoat, acts as a substitute for inherent violence. These approaches take as their premiss violence itself as a constitutive element in humanity. This is something they share with Bataille, although in many ways Bataille was less crudely essentialist in his understanding of the dialectic of taboo and transgression. Most anthropologists have criticized Girard (though not Burkert) for poor scholarship, and on empirical grounds this work does not seem any more acceptable than that of Bataille as the basis for any general theory of sacrifice. A further criticism has been made of their attempt to abstract violence as a kind of primitive beginning separated off from the necessary equivocations of ethics that result from contextualization (e.g. Rosaldo 1987, Alexiou 1990, Rose 1992: 135–52).

It is not, however, necessary to involve such primitivist conceptualization of violence in order to accept that violence has an essential place in sacrifice as the mechanism for the destruction of the sacrificial victim. This potentiality may, however, be ignored in many societies where butchery is simply mundane technology. More recently, Bloch (1992) provides a rather better-grounded consideration for understanding the relation of violence to other aspects of such rituals. He explores the manner by which in some societies the violence absorbed through the contact with the divine is then appropriated in post-sacrificial reconstitution by that society, sometimes as aggression against others. This is one, and there may be a number of other, plausible arguments which provide us with a logic by which to comprehend the use made by various societies of the play of violence in sacrifice. But it does not follow that these should be generalized into some necessity for either recognizing or absorbing/dissipating some essentialized violence assumed to be inherent to sacrifice.

In most cases it is the very totality of sacrifice, as insisted upon by Hubert and Mauss, that acts to repudiate this potential of violence, which is absorbed within the rite. As they note, the later stages of sacrifice employ various mean to 'cool off' or 'tame' the sacralized powers that have been unleashed in the sacrificial act. What is significant perhaps is that the theme of violence, in particular the way it is portrayed by Girard, has become amongst the most influential theories of sacrifice outside anthropology, its popularity having, one suspects, more to do with the desire to find in violence some basic form of authenticity to humankind rather than any serious concern with the nature of traditional sacrifice. Violence, as a theme in sacrifice, then becomes part of what might be called the abstracted discourse of sacrifice. This would imply that Girard and similar writings may be taken, not so much as accounts of sacrifice as a ritual practice, but rather as showing the degree to which contemporary society (and others before us) have abstracted from sacrifice a discourse which emphasizes, or exploits, the violence that may be found within sacrificial rituals. It is this abstraction of violence as the discourse of sacrifice which will be returned to in the next section.

Shopping as a Sacrifical Rite

The literature upon sacrifice provides the other pieces of the jig-saw that were required for this theory of shopping. The remainder of this chapter comprises a three-part narrative which employs all these loose pieces of argument and evidence and puts them together in order to create a theory derived from the juxtaposition of shopping and sacrifice. The three sections constitute the theory of shopping referred to in the title of this essay. I do not expect, however, that every part of this argument will be equally convincing, and the third chapter which follows is therefore intended to provide further arguments to justify and to consider the consequences of this theory.

Stage One: a Vision of Excess

What is not often stressed, but seems of critical importance in understanding sacrifice, is that this rite often represents the moment at which the previous labour of accumulation is turned into the expenditure of the resources accumulated. Sacrifice as an act of consumption must always evoke the spending of what has been created or gathered. In many cases this is the end point of the labour of production, of growing crops and raising livestock. In other societies it is the capture of victims through war and raiding that must be acknowledged. This relationship is most evident in first-fruit sacrifices where there is a seasonal element to the growing of foods so that a moment can be defined in the year at which production turns into consumption. But this transformation is also acknowledged in the concern often shown for the quality of the resources that should be used in sacrifice. As Bataille noted, in many sacrificial rites considerable stress is laid upon the high value of the sacrificial victim. These are not merely the products of labour, they are the perfect products, the unblemished objects that by their very perfection speak to the aid of gods and spirits as essential to the success of production. In the sheer perfection of the sacrificial victim may be found an echo of sacrifice as a return to the deity of that which can only exist through the blessings of the deity.

In first-fruit ceremonials, it is the moment when consumption is made possible, when the first-born have been delivered and the crops have ripened, before expenditure is really able to get going, that these goods are creamed off and given to the deity. Sacrifice then represents an insistence upon the importance of the sacred being interposed in the transformation of productive forms into consumption. In some societies this is widened to make virtually all acts of consumption of particular edibles first and foremost a sacrificial act. As many grounds as possible are found for turning consumption into an activity which constitutes a relationship to the divine.

It is very common for societies to enact a form of prohibition on the initial consumption of that which they have produced. Munn (1986) argues that a similar prohibition is central to the much used anthropological case study of the Kula ring.[40] Immediate consumption of that which one produces, means that the products cannot be used for expanding the symbolic place-time – what she calls the 'fame' – of either the individuals or the society. Only after products are used in complex inter-island exchanges which build extensive networks within which the producers gain renown should that which has been exchanged for island produce be finally consumed. Her argument applies still more to the transcendent realm. Sacrifice here becomes a kind of Kula with the gods. Mere consumption would in a sense reduce the producer to mere pragmatism. We produce merely to eat. By making sure that from its very inception consumption is subject to the dialectical enhancement of society, a process in which the object is split apart and an element used to constitute the divine, this fate is avoided. This is certainly not a profitless activity as implied by the logic of Bataille's argument. On the contrary, the power that is thereby unleashed is far greater than could ever be hoped for from the mere accumulation of mundane resources. The goods that are spent in sacrifice are well spent. The logic is not one of economics, however, but of objectification.[41]

The implication of this perspective on sacrifice is, however, that there is implicit in the act another vision of expenditure. This is the very idea that such goods and resources might well be frittered away in mere human use without being involved in sacrifice. Furthermore, in as much as sacrifice is based on human obeisance before the divine, the failure to perform sacrifice takes on an element of refusal, a transgressive liberation from religious obligation. The constant theme in ancient literatures is of human endeavours that go wrong because people failed to carry out sacrifices that were mandatory. The reiteration of this message itself confirms the temptation to freedom from such obligations, that is to use such resources for profane purposes.

This is the context for the vision of sacrifice held by Bataille and in different ways resurrected by a recent stress on violence and excess in the literature on sacrifice. What is noteworthy is that this literature is generally condemned by those with a strong commitment to the scholarly study of actual sacrifice but has proved immensely seductive and attractive despite this. This suggests that it constitutes a discourse of sacrifice that is not the same as actual sacrifice taken as a whole but is instead a common starting-point for the imagination of sacrifice in the abstract. Bataille was surely closer to the mark than Girard or Burkert. It is not violence *per se* that is found in sacrifice but the violence of consumption as expenditure. Sacrifice may well evoke a vision of excess, of violent expenditure, but it is one with which sacrifice must take issue. In some cases this may be through sacrifice itself commencing with a spectacle of violent expenditure.

The very definition of sacrifice, that which separates it from other acts of consecration, is that it is based upon consumption. Sacrifice is the violent destruction of some otherwise useful resource in an act of expenditure. Bataille's work is critical to understanding the way this can be abstracted as a discourse of sacrifice, which focuses the imagination on consumption as the destruction of resources. Bataille reveals the consequences of taking up the cosmological implications of destructive consumption. Indeed for him, in a secular world it is expenditure alone that can evoke the transcendent purposes of life. Bataille, whose reasoning at heart is almost always dialectical, sees the annihilation of forms (most fully in death itself) as the proper way in which life itself is constituted.

Bataille interposes here a vision of consumption which has no point other than the glory of pure expenditure. The focus upon death forces us to abstract the essence of life, as in Judaism where blood is radically separated from the remainder of the corporeal as representing life in and of itself, to become a substance that can only be consumed by God. Recent theories of sacrifice have once again returned to the significance of a vision of violence as constitutive of society. In effect they extract from the earlier focus upon the totality of the ritual what is seen as its defining moment, the act of destruction.

Rather than rejecting the literature on violence in sacrifice, I am simply shifting it from its intention of accounting for sacrifice *per se* and transforming it into an initial vision encapsulated within a discourse about sacrifice. It becomes the starting-point or premiss behind sacrifice. If we were to grant that destruction is the very essence of sacrifice then it would represent precisely the liberating transgression that Bataille celebrates. Yet the idea that most religious authorities spent their time encouraging an act of transgression is to say the least unlikely. Most religious traditions are concerned not to realize this vision but to negate it. The tight technical constraints upon how exactly sacrifice should take place and the rigorous control of important sacrifices suggest that, while it may have to evoke this discourse of transgression, the point of the ritual is to negate it as a possibility and ensure that sacrifice is turned back into an ordered relationship to the divine.

Transgression may be represented by either the mere profane consumption of goods or by the violent destruction of victims as spectacle. This outcome is prevented when sacrificial ritual is

allowed to run its course, since the rite has the effect of transforming potential transgression into something quite different.
Transgression is tamed and suppressed within a divinely constituted order of the world. This conclusion becomes evident when
we return to the perspective granted by the analysis of sacrifice
by Hubert and Mauss. For the early stages of sacrifice their
emphasis is on the movement from the profane to the sacred and
the technology involved in making both victim and sacrificer
appropriate. The first stage is simply the extraction of materials
and action from the profane world to prepare for entry into the
realm of the sacred. But Hubert and Mauss insist that sacrifice
must also be seen as a whole, and it will be shown in the subsequent two sections that by the time we have moved through
the second stage and into the third stage of sacrifice, what begins
as an image of violence or transgression becomes a rite devoted
entirely to the re-establishment of conventional order and structure in the world. By acknowledging the presence of a discourse
that raises another possibility we will come to understand this as
a practice which negates its own discourse.

To understand the cosmological significance of shopping in
North London requires a remarkably similar point of departure.
The premiss of shopping, like that of sacrifice, is that it is the
precise moment when everything that had focused upon the
accumulation of resources is about to turn into the moment when
those same resources are expended. It refers backwards to all the
labour that has gone into working for the money to be spent,
which may carry with it the resentments, the achievements and a
host of other experiences of work. All of this prior labour is first
reduced to the abstraction of money. All that concrete action
becomes mere paper notes and coins – these days often a piece
of plastic – that seem to harbour such potential but also seem
such a fragile monument to what had gone into its production.
For those who do not work but live on state benefits there is just
as much ambivalence, potential mixed with resentment, asserted
rights and stigmatized guilt, bound up in what is faced as a quite
frightful substance – money. In such circumstances, it is hardly
surprising that money should itself appear, as Simmel argued
(1978), to be more philosophical than material substance. Money

by its very abstraction from labour already seems to objectify potentially transgressive forms, floating away from its proper grounding in society.

It is not surprising either than many societies produced a radical symbolic split between production and expenditure, as when production is fully gendered as males who will not be associated with shopping, and consumption becomes viewed as a purely female activity, a female whose labour is unvalorized except where it expresses her agency as expenditure.[42] In such a context women become the agents who expend what men are understood to have produced. Women then take on the symbolic burden of expenditure. Much of the aggressive misogyny that characterized the period of the 1950s and 1960s, prior to feminism, was directed as resentment against the woman shopper, who turned the seriousness of labour into the trivia of consumption.

Though feminism has made this relationship more subtle, it remains the case that the fear and ambivalence that reside in money by virtue of its abstraction becomes released through the imagination of shopping as an act of spending money that turns production and state benefits into consumption. At the precise moment of this transformation there arises a vision, which becomes the premiss for the act of shopping, and which has been termed here the discourse of shopping. Its substance is barely different from that which Bataille and others have seen in the premiss of sacrifice. It is a vision of pure excess. In this vision all the hard work and labour that went into accumulating money is fantasized as being destroyed in a sheer exhilarating bout of transgressive freedom. The abstract idea of shopping is clearly one of pointlessness; it is shopping for the sake of it, for items that are not necessities, but themselves stand for profligacy. The discourse of shopping is purely destructive, a marvellous envisaging of complete waste. It captures the transgressive potentiality of money itself, explored by Simmel and others, as asocial liberation from considerations of particularity. It barely matters what is purchased as long as the money is spent. This becomes evident in the social fascination with shopaholics, but more importantly is foundational to the very concept of shopping as an abstracted discourse.

Despite feminism, the transgressive element is extended by the idea of the pure profligate shopper being female, precisely because the female remains the gender which bears the mantle of responsibility for actual or potential households. The fear as to whether the female can be trusted to act as the self-abnegating consumer is given poignancy by an almost ecstatic vision of this female luxuriating in the manifold pleasures of a shopping mall in complete disregard of any kind of larger responsibility. The degree to which shopping thrills as destructive consumption is dependent upon the degree to which its agent, the shopper, is the same person who is supposed to objectify pure self-sacrifice as a housewife living on behalf of her household. In this vision spending becomes a goal in and of itself, de-contextualized from social life. The shopper is imagined engaged in pure self-indulgence following the dictates of individualized hedonism. Shopping comes to objectify a form of absolute freedom that fantasizes a separation off from being defined by any social relations and obligations. What informants constantly called 'real' shopping, the shopping that they feel I ought to be studying, must study, that is shopping which is never real, is an imagined act of blissful annihilation of the socially constituted self in favour of a self constructed through the process of individualistic hedonism.

For this vision, consumption must be trivial, and the giant malls must stand in our ideology as symbols of sheer emptiness, crammed full of pure ephemera that have the power to dissipate the seriousness of labour into an objectifying of nothing. The notion of primitive violence in sacrifice is overtrumped by the idea or ideal of civilization, that most sophisticated development of human kind, blown away in an orgy of spending. A favourite image is of high culture such as art torn asunder by vulgar merchandising – the Velázquez tea-tray, classic Rome turned into a shop front. The academic theory of postmodernism provides admirable service to our need for a vision of destructive consumption as pointless waste, which is precisely why, although I suspect it is almost entirely an illusion, so many academics seem devoted to representing our age as postmodern.

Although there may be potential analogies with sexuality used to project similar kinds of freedom (e.g. Miller 1994: 113–25), there was little evidence in the ethnography for the presence of any element that could be closely identified with the erotic, with violence, with death or any of the senses of destructive consumption that so exercised Bataille. Yet the potential for a relationship between these three is evident, and one need only turn to newspapers to find it realized. The sheer exhilaration and exhaustion of the fantasized bout of pure shopping easily evokes the same sense of annihilation of the self as is imagined for sexual climax. Of course, most actual sex isn't much like this vision of excess either, but it is at the level of fantasy that the relationship holds. It is a voyeuristic vision which is most evident in that it dominates contemporary journalism where violence, sex and shopping comprise a kind of triumvirate of thrill.

Within the same modern discourse of shopping there is also a version which generalizes from a fantasy of individual consumption to that of universal consumption. This is most fully apparent in the rhetoric of the Green movement where it takes on an image of violence that again evokes the discourse of sacrifice. Here consumerism becomes the primary image for the destruction of the world. Consumption represents a violent rape of 'mother earth's' natural resources through mindless destruction, such that commerce itself becomes subsumed by consumption. Indeed in this rhetoric the consumer is no longer the duped victim of capitalism, rather it is the consumers themselves who by their irresponsibility pillage the world and exhaust it in their insatiable desires, thereby conniving with capitalism as the means to their ends. Despite these rhetorics, it seems that in shopping as in sacrifice these visions are negated by a second stage of the ritual almost before they have a chance to be formulated.

Stage Two: Smoke Ascends to the Divinity

It is quite possible that particular regimes of sacrifice may extend the idea of violence and destruction and make them a paramount element within sacrifice. These may, as suggested by Girard (1977), incorporate anxieties and psychological tensions developed within other areas of life. In rather more cases it is likely that it is the very fear of that other use of resources, their transgressive potential, that leads the religious functionaries to make sacrifice into a spectacle of violence, but one that entices the populace back into religiosity and the orders sanctified by religion. In their constant warning about the dangers of neglecting proper sacrifice priests are trying to ensure that the vision of transgressive destruction is transmuted within the performance of sacrificial ritual into its opposite. But there is no necessity here. Most sacrifice is mundane, and violence may play little or no role in it. Rather, sacrifice may become a rather pedestrian form of expenditure that secures a relationship with the divine and which in turn makes that expenditure far more productive and efficacious.

Where sacrifice is carried out with sufficient regularity and including sufficiently minor acts, it becomes quickly suffused into part of ordinary practice. This is important to the interpretation. While many societies had occasion for spectacular sacrifices that might be the climax of a religious cycle of the year, most such societies also used sacrifice on a much more mundane and regular basis. Detienne (1989: 1) notes: 'First of all, we see in the Greeks a society in which the basic ritual acts in daily practice are of a sacrificial type.' Furthermore, 'All consumable meat comes from ritually slaughtered animals, and the butcher who sheds the animals' blood bears the same functional name as the sacrificer posted next to the bloody altar' (ibid.: 3). Any significant political act in ancient Greece depended on an initial sacrifice. Similarly, in reading the Jewish Pentateuch the sheer ubiquity of sacrifice is evident, not just as part of almost every aspect of the ritual year from first fruits to atonement, but for a wide range of more mundane *ad hoc* purposes. So in comparing shopping to sacrifice we are comparing the main form of expenditure and consumption in our society with one of the main forms of expenditure and consumption in many other societies.

Bataille was wrong, above all, because his vision of sacrifice was one of pointlessness that thereby repudiates utility, but in traditional sacrifice, just as in most shopping, the dominant concern is to achieve specific purposes – which are often pragmatic and practical. Most sacrifice, like most shopping, was at one level a way of spending things in order to gain other things. But neither shopping nor sacrifice are simply pragmatic acts of expenditure for profit. What is crucial to their definition is that they achieve their practical logic only by passing through sacred rites which ensure that before the practical aims can be achieved they are first used to sanctify and sustain objects of devotion.

The crux of the ritual in both cases is the separation of the sacrificed into two elements, one of which is given up to the transcendent and the other returns back to the mundane. In the case of sacrifice it may be the sweet savour of the offering arising as smoke. In modern Hindu worship it is usually *prasad* or a tokenistic element that is presented before the deity. This occurs through either the burning or at least the presentation of the sacrificial offering at the altar. The definition of sacrifice given by Valeri for Hawaii exemplifies this stress on the sacrifice creating a relationship between two divided-off aspects of the whole.

> Each part of the offering, which is a double of the sacrifier, signifies a different state of his. The part that remains with the god signified the state of the sacrifier when he is intently consciousness of what the god stands for: the concept of the sacrifier's subject. This level of consciousness was in the foreground when the sacrifier's attention was entirely focused on the god and the offering entirely consecrated to him. The part that is detached from the god signifies the state of the sacrifier's consciousness when his attention is redirected towards the concrete world. (Valeri 1985: 71–2)

This separates off the second stage which is the constitution of the divine through the establishment of a relationship, from what will be described below as the third stage based on the return of sacrifice to its implications for the profane world and the social order. It is the ascent of the smoke, the release of the blood or whichever element goes directly to the gods that tends to constitute the central rite within sacrifice. It is this act which ensures that the abstract vision of expenditure is transmuted into a symbolic or actual giving up of resources to the divine.

In shopping, as in sacrifice, one starts with a vision of excess. In the contemporary world there are grounds for considering this to have become a global vision since journalism and other media have proved such a powerful transnational and transcultural force that there are certain universalizing visions that have colonized almost every regional niche. This was one of the main reasons why I felt justified in treating the North London street as a single homogenized and normative category, notwithstanding the fact that it was neither a community nor homogeneous in background. At the level of the discourse of shopping these differences seemed to count for very little as compared to the uniformity of expressions about the abstract nature of shopping as expenditure.

In actual shopping, as in actual sacrifice, there may be times and places where the discourse of excessive expenditure is manifested in practice. But for most people these remain within set frames that impose clear boundaries, such as leisure shopping on holiday, the treat within a shopping expedition or the luxury and indulgence that make an event special, or, as in courtship, a relationship special. The treat, in particular, by helping to define the recipient of shopping and often the experience of individuality, is crucial in determining the aura of the remainder of shopping. The setting of excessive expenditure within such frames has the effect of taming it, and rendering the bulk of shopping part of something quite different. It allows for the formation of the second stage of shopping analogous to the second stage of sacrifice.

This second stage should act as the negation of the vision of excess. For shopping to become analogous to sacrifice it must go through the same kind of splitting process that was argued to represent the central rite of sacrifice. In this case it must be a split between the concern for the profane or social consequences of the act which comes to constitute the third stage and the constitution of a transcendent goal to which shopping is dedicated which must be equivalent to the divine recipient of sacrifice. The 'smoke' or essence of shopping as a ritual must be separated off from the mundane elements and consequences of shopping.

Based on ethnographic observation, there can be little doubt as to what plays the analogous role as the central ritual transformation of shopping. Most shopping expeditions begin as acts of intended expenditure, but the actual practice of shopping, its skills, its labour and its primary goals, become increasingly directed to the possibility of thrift. By the time the act of shopping is completed the experience has been transformed into an ethos that is the very negation of expenditure, being thoroughly absorbed in the vision of money saved.

To be assigned this place as the cosmological pivot of shopping, thrift must be removed from its mere presence as skill and technology. The fact that somebody pays less for a commodity is not itself significant. The emphasis could still be on expenditure, that is on the fact that Sheila spends £2 pounds but not £3. But thrift turns money not spent into money saved. What emerges is not the image of Sheila spending £2, but of Sheila saving £1. The 'value' of the commodity commonly becomes not what it costs but what it saved. Only then does the act of shopping become a negation of the vision of expenditure. This conclusion based on the ethnography of shoppers was found to be fully supported by the observation of contemporary commerce and the efforts made to attract custom by making retail into a site for the practice of thrift. It has already been shown that the concern for thrift is irrespective of income and need. But this in turn leads to a central, as yet unanswered, question. For whom or for what is all of this being done?

Why is it so important, that even for the wealthy, the experience of shopping should be one of saving? The act of spending is clearly directed to particular subjects; items of clothing, for example, are almost always *ad hominem*. Food is either for specific individuals or feeding the household more generally. Furnishing is directed to the home, but the home as a clear material entity. When it comes to saving, however, the beneficiary is rather vaguer. It is possible to elicit some intentions behind saving. For example, a woman teacher of West African origin when asked who or what she was saving for replied 'For my child, for us, in case one day we get unemployed', but the question of thrift rarely elicits an answer even of this specificity. Most people would have to think long and hard to give an answer, not because the question is hard, but because they see the question as too easy. It's too obvious that one would want to save money. It is understood as simply a good thing. But the comparative literature on thrift (see chapter 3) demonstrates that the academic problem of enunciating this 'good thing' is by no means simple.

Thrift is a form of deferment. It includes the provision that the money saved now could be spent later, which might represent merely a husbanding of resources, but both the comparative and the contextual evidence suggests that it is usually more than this. By representing an extreme case the elderly are important here. There were cases of the most impoverished elderly who were amongst the most obsessive about saving money. But this money was not used to improve their own standard of living by being spent on themselves at a later date. It was more often seen as the basis for buying large presents for descendants. This in turn might be seen as an attempt by the lonely to buy attention, in the hope that great-grandchildren will pay them a visit. It may be partly that, but if so it was not often a success and would have to be seen as either a desperate measure or the persistence of people wilfully ignorant of a string of past failures. It is more convincing to see this thrift in terms of what the elderly actually do, which is to give gifts to their descendants irrespective of any actual reciprocal gestures by that particular descendant. Thrift then is turned into the constitution of the sense of descent line, that is a devotional gift to the future, which is for the elderly increasingly serving as the legitimacy of the past. It is perhaps a vestigial remains of the sense of transcendence and immortality that is represented by 'the house' as a descent line (see chapter 3).

If this explanation is accepted, then the most significant implication is that the descent line is most fully objectified by the act of thrift rather than any actual descendants. For some of the elderly the encounter with these descendants may be very rare – once a year at Christmas, even less if the children live abroad. But the presence of the following generations is reconstituted on an almost daily basis by the act of thrift itself. The implication is that thrift is entirely misunderstood if it is thought of as a means to an end. Thrift itself is the end, since thrift is the way in which the other is objectified as a presence. In the extreme case the other is merely an excuse for thrift as a mechanism for constituting a transcendent goal for life. Of course, for the non-believer this is exactly what is happening in sacrifice. While for the believer sacrifice is a means towards reaching God, for the non-believer God is merely a creation of the process which therefore should be seen as an end in itself.

The elderly represent this logic with particular clarity, but the argument holds for most shoppers to some extent or other. Teenagers or those 'in search of themselves' are the least concerned with thrift, but once the stage is reached when people wish to be in a relationship of love then thrift can come into play, whether or not there is an object of love. In some ways the absence of objects of love makes things easier, since the actual partner or child is often so far from the idealized object that they have to be 'unthought' in order to be reconstituted as the proper recipients of love. This is the case when the woman who sees her goal as housewife has almost to ignore an actual family, which shows next to no appreciation of her labour, in order to maintain her sense of self-worth based on the self-sacrifice of thrift.

Thrift then requires no particular object of concern. It is a highly generalized, extremely vague sense of deferment. As a form of deferment thrift becomes the Kantian aesthetic translated into everyday action – a refusal of immediate desire in order to make life a bit more beautiful than it otherwise would be. So just as Trobriand Islanders grow practical gardens for their food which are at the same time the idealized gardens secured by ritual and magic (Malinowski 1935, Gell 1992), so practical shopping is also an idealized activity whose sanctity is secured by the ritual transformation into saving. We would be quite wrong to assume that thrift is some hard-nosed economizing opposed to such idealized visions. This is hardly likely when shoppers don't even know the prices of the goods they buy, or whether they have actually spent more through searching for savings. What matters is that the general sense of being thrifty becomes abstracted from a specific act of saving.

Thrift is not just an aesthetic but one with a particular form. The aesthetic of thrift starts with a principle which could be termed centripetal (as opposed to centrifugal). It is an attempt to retain resources within the household. As an attitude to the world it moves to draw things inwards and prevent their escape. As such it is part of a more general centripetal aesthetic, directed to keeping a core to the domestic world. The aesthetics of thrift have become evident through other studies I have conducted on the aesthetics of furnishing and decoration of the home itself, where this same sense of enclosure and retention can be discerned (e.g. Miller 1988, 1994: 206–19). Even men's traditionally more profligate outer directed spending is being swept back into this centripetality through the rise of the DIY warehouses and the garden centres, that gives them a role in spending that draws them back into the domestic. Indeed, most spending is directed inwards, either furnishing the house or feeding and clothing the household. Once the internal boundaries of the domestic are established, then the money saved can be used in public gifts that expand the fame or continuity of the household. The most legitimate spending is that which goes down the generations to children's birthdays, education or to grandchildren.

Thrift is instrumental in creating the general sense that there is some more important goal than immediate gratification, that there is some transcendent force or future purpose that justifies the present deferment. In the absence of any belief in a deity, thrift transcends particular relationships and rises to a higher level that evokes something above and beyond their immediacy. What thrift thereby achieves is made more evident when we return to its starting-point, which was the discourse of shopping. This discourse was understood as the self-consciousness of the negative potential of shopping as the mere dissipation of resources, without these being used first to establish a transcendent object or purpose to life. So just as sacrifice is in practice the negation of that vision of excess identified by Bataille, so shopping centres upon thrift as the effective means to negate an extremely similar vision of excess in consumption. What Bataille never seems to have envisaged is that it could be such a mundane economizing that is most effective at repudiating mere utilitarianism, rather than some massive gesture of destruction. In both shopping and sacrifice this constitutes the second and central stage to the process. In both cases it involves a separation from the concerns of social and profane purposes and draws one upwards to what Valeri saw as a consciousness focused upon the divine. But the third stage in turn negates the second by returning the vision back to the specific objects of love.

Stage Three: the Sacrificial Meal

The last part of the quotation from Valeri that was used to describe the second stage is reproduced here together with the section which followed from it in the original.

> The part that is detached from the god signifies the state of the sacrifier's consciousness when his attention is redirected towards the concrete world. Eating this part creates a transition from the previous states of consciousness to the ordinary one and at the same time subordinates the later to the former, since the two parts are metonymically related. The eating also marks the effect of this subordination: the reproduction of the sacrifier's relationship with his group and of his ability to act in it. (Valeri 1985: 71–2)

The third stage of sacrifice is marked then by a turning away from the relationship to the divine and a return to the social relations of profane society and the social consequences of sacrifice. As Hubert and Mauss argued, this return to society is saturated with the consequences of the process through which it has passed. Indeed, many of the final rites may include rituals of desacralization in order to ward off the dangers of too powerful or sometimes malignant elements of the sacred that remain after the relationship to the divine has been sundered.

The research that has been most clearly orientated to this third and final stage of sacrifice is that of Detienne and Vernant (1989) and their associates' analyses of the sacrificial meal. Much of their work is based on the reconstruction of the specific rituals involved in classifying the parts of the sacrificial victim and ensuring that they are cooked and eaten in a manner that is appropriate to their symbolic status. This in turn is related to the re-analysis of key Greek myths which, they argue, provide the legitimation and rationale behind these particular divisions of the sacrifice.

But the emphasis upon classification in regard to the sacrificial victim is only intended to reaffirm the centrality of sacrifice to another classification, which is the social order of Greek society. Their studies take their place in a line of anthropological enquiry stretching from Durkheim to Bourdieu, in which it is the transference of taxonomic order that most effectively reproduces society as a sanctified formation. It is then in this final action of consumption that the power of the transcendent is used to confirm and reify the social relations of the group. In particular, forms of hierarchy and difference are ritually re-established by the division of the sacrificial animal between consumers, who may or may not have participated in the sacrificial act itself. In many cases, this is used to affirm the separation of a priestly caste, but also of nobles and of gender and other social divisions. It follows that one of the main consequences of sacrifice is the sanctification of social order. This brings us close to the main conclusion of the feminist critique of consumption. Consumption practices are condemned primarily because they act as a conservative force reifying the given asymmetries in the social order.

Although my study was specifically that of shopping, shopping is rarely an isolated act of provisioning. Most commonly it is just one moment in the larger concern of an individual for the household. In the ethnography it was clear that this responsibility pertained to a wide gamut of provisioning. With hardly any exception it was a female who was responsible for the clothing of the children, and to a surprising extent females were also the main buyers or at least the initiators of buying of clothing for their partners. Similarly, although the purchase of major household goods is usually made by a couple, this is conceptualized as a purchase by 'the household'. This concept subsumes and removes the sense of the individuality of the actual purchasers. In our larger study of shopping centres it was found that the key image the centre used to attract shoppers was based on an ideology of family shopping, notwithstanding the clear evidence that very few people actually liked to shop with their families. This was because the concept of family as a household stood for a much wider set of values than individualized family members (see Miller et al. in press ch. 5).

In the second stage of these rites, thrift has been used to construct an imaginary and ideal household created as the objectification of the larger values and goals of the shopper, which thereby stands in relation to shopping as God does to sacrifice. In the third stage this imaginary household is replaced by the actual members of families, but as in all social relations these retain a sense of the idealized relationship and the individual as standing for idealized role 'child' or 'wife', as well as all those particular traits that make up the specific character of the person and the relationship. The continued role of imagined and idealized traits brings to the third stage that sanctity that was created during the second stage of the devotional rite.

The most fully documented component of this wider context to which the proceeds of shopping are subsequently put is in the feeding of the family. DeVault (1991) provides the best analysis of the link between shopping and feeding, although there are several precedents to her study, such as those by Charles and Kerr (1988) and Murcott (1983), that are equally adamant about the continued subsumption of the individual female provider in her relationship to the household in both Britain and the United States (see also p. 37 above). This is often exemplified in her lack of interest in cooking if it is merely to provide for herself, because there is no one else present in the house.

Feeding the family then stands for the modern act of consumption in an analogous relationship to feeding the community in ancient sacrifice. It is the final stage, where that which has not been given up to the transcendent in the form of saving money returns as the sanctified purchases which are then given out to the recipients as the remains of the sacrificial act. If at all possible, some of the eating should represent a collective act that symbolizes the continuity of the group, and the relationships within it, even if this is no more than a couple eating together, or the annual Christmas meal. Many housewives expressed their frustration at the decline of family meals. In our society just as much as in ancient society we can see the two main effects to which Detienne and Vernant have drawn attention. The first is the transference of efficacy from the transcendent realm back into the profane and the second the re-establishment of social order through acts of distribution and consumption.

Indeed, thanks to DeVault's work, 'Feeding the Family' could well stand as the key symbol of this final act of sacrifice. This is why DeVault found it so much of a problem to assert her feminist perspective within her own enquiry into contemporary American meals. DeVault's analysis depends upon taking the act of feeding families as work, that is as the sum total of all the effort put into, not only shopping, but thinking through what would make an appropriate meal, and preparing and cooking the meal. As a feminist she is affronted by the evidence that her informants would not view this activity as work, but constantly refer back to an ideology that institutes devotion as the sole legitimate grounds and criteria by which this work is done.

The 'problem' faced by DeVault is answered by what might be called the 'solution' which in chapter 3 is associated with the work of Weiner (1992). This is the evidence that women as a gender are used to objectify love, and a love that stands defined as that humanity which will not be reduced to equivalence or exchange. In the third stage of shopping as sacrifice the element of transcendence that stood as generalized devotion in the form of thrift is turned into the specific expression of devotional love directed between woman as the continued instrument of love and those for whom she has brought back the sacrificial remains in the form of purchases. Love here is the dialectical transformation of the generality of devotion back into particularity. Having become sanctified through her agency in the self-sacrifice of thrift, she returns with the blessing of love to her family. As seen in the ethnographic section with which this essay began, she expresses her love and devotion to the same degree to which she is able to tease out the very specific and often transient desires of each individualized object of love. She buys this particular brand or flavour, in relation to her sense of not only what the individual wants, but her reasoning as to what would improve that individual. In practice the two may be compromised in the form of what she can get that wretched object of love to actually eat! DeVault's ability to extract every last ounce of calculation, compromise, frustration and juggling of demands from the practice of housewifery becomes then a testament to the skills of love.

It is the objectification of love as female in general that enhances the ability of particular females to transfer the sense of transcendence – the goal in life that rises beyond mere living – and bring this into daily practice, where it is recognized as 'devotion'. The sense of the female as devotee, the agent who reconstitutes a moral order, is enhanced by the use of shopping to negate another vision, that of the female as pure transgressive spendthrift abnegating any sense of responsibility. Equally, the more the male is objectified as pure utility and function the more the female encompasses that which is defined as irreducible to calculation. The evidence from the ethnography of shopping is that this remains very much the norm. Even where males are being constantly reintroduced into the arena of shopping on the grounds of equality, they find strategies of distancing themselves or at least of treating shopping as merely a pragmatic and utilitarian act. This was particularly clear in the case of clothing. Although there is the vision of the dandy and the male with a keen interest in style, in practice most males conformed to a more conservative image of buying only to replace items. Typically they define a shop such as Marks & Spencer (whose clothing has a very different image from that of its food department) as neutral and standard. This means the male can buy clothing which he regards as pure utility, embodying nothing, and reducing shopping to a kind of minimalist symbol of utility. Men can thereby shop without care, leaving the embodiment of care in shopping as a largely female preserve. Any weekday trip down the London Underground will give testimony to the continued domination of a male sartorial ideal of unexpressive normativity.

If women then become the medium that transfers sacred efficacy from sacrifice to devotion, then the second point of Detienne and Vernant's analysis works equally well in the North London context. Again, the point can be returned to a consideration of DeVault. The reason her work is so entirely successful as a feminist critique is that it follows from all that has been said that she has identified precisely the mechanisms which reproduce social inequality and the exploitation of women's labour. It is the very sacred nature of love as devotion which creates the immensely conservative resistance to DeVault's feminist critique of gender. In ancient Greece the act of sacrifice which began with a vision of transgression, freedom and excess ends with a picture of normative morality and confirmed social order literally enshrined through the dynamics of the sacrificial act. Shopping as cosmology becomes thereby a conservative preservation of the orders of inequality. Caught within the ancient logic of sacrifice, feminism becomes tantamount to telling a mother that she should not take her love for her children for granted. It is noticeable that for all the critique of normative marriage implied in DeVault there is very little attempt by her to challenge a mother's love. To that extent we can conclude that for all the pressures of secularization and the Enlightenment, the desire to subsume the individual in acts of devotion remains at the heart of modern female identity, even if the ideal that 'God is Love' has tended to be transformed within the experience of the contemporary family into 'Love is God'. It is to this historical transformation of the subjects of devotion that the third chapter is addressed.

3

Subjects and Objects
of Devotion

The heat of the last section has been used to fuse my various ingredients into a theory. But what kind of theory? Is this a mere soufflé made largely of hot air, hopefully enjoyable but of little substance, or is there depth and consequence that will be sustaining? I have carried out archaeological and ethnographic fieldwork in a number of different regions where animal sacrifice is still a common practice. As a result I have attended perhaps hundreds of such events involving animals from chickens and pigs to water buffalo, in regions from the Solomon Islands, through India and Indonesia to Trinidad. Being squeamish, I may not have observed these as closely as I should have done, but I think I can bear clear testimony to the fact that none of them looked much like the act of shopping.

The creation of a juxtaposition between shopping and sacrifice through an analysis of similarities in their underlying structure, while acknowledging diversity from this generalized structure in both cases, may serve many purposes. As an argument it may be mere analogy or may imply direct historical replacement of one by the other. It may be a weak analogy or a strong one. This chapter will examine the links between these two activities and suggest that they amount to much more than mere analogy. By examining the background to some of the key concepts used, such as love and thrift, it will try to be more precise about what is implied by the idea of smoke rising, or devotion offered, when these terms are taken from sacrifice and applied to shopping.

The primary articulation of shopping and sacrifice will be accomplished through a consideration of the development of various subjects and objects of devotion. Initially, these are set against each other. First, a consideration is given to the subjects of devotion: gods, patriarchy and infants, and the main contemporary expression of that devotion as love. Following this, the focus is turned upon the objects of devotion as in inalienable possessions, thrift, the house and finally supermarket commodities. By the conclusion, however, the attempt will have been made to see the relationship between subjects and objects as a dialectic, such that each is used to constitute the other in the manner suggested by theories of objectification.[43]

I cannot be sure how far readers will be persuaded by these links, some of which are more conjectural than others. For this reason I would start with the assertion that even if they are entirely rejected and all that was left of the previous two chapters was the construction of an analogy between shopping and sacrifice, then the exercise might still be justified. The benefits of even a weak form of analogy are most evident in relation to the understanding of contemporary shopping. The literature on shopping has been a mixture of the dismissive and the functional, the former when consideration has been given to the shopper and the latter when consideration is given to retailing. Most commercially orientated work is devoted to classifying types of shoppers in order to assist targeting of consumers through marketing. Many other studies concentrate almost entirely on the techniques by which business manipulates shoppers.[44] Recent sociological discussion has been closely aligned with the journalistic and the discourse of shopping which applies also to the shoppers themselves. All three tend to use shopping as a convenient symbol for condemning ourselves as some kind of postmodern superficiality devoted to mindless materialism.[45] Shopping as a topic has not suffered from neglect, but rather from being constantly drawn upon as a convenient symbol for a larger and largely unhelpful attempt to characterize the *Zeitgeist*.

At the very least then, an analogy with sacrifice should open up the possibility that shopping is a practice that might have ritual structure, that might be involved in the creation of value and relationships and that might manifest elements of cosmology, even if not those that I have argued for in this particular theory. Analogy here becomes a kind of intellectual crowbar that is intended to prise shopping out of the niche within which it is conventionally housed and permit a very different perspective to emerge. It is also possible that this analogy may as a by-product also stimulate a rather more empathetic appreciation of the significance of sacrifice.

But I am by no means satisfied with mere analogy. I do intend a stronger argument and one with more sustained consequence. There are not just grounds for making the analogy but reasons why the analogy should work well. The discussion of specific objects and subjects of devotion will be used to claim both historical continuities and reasons why a close structural analogy might still pertain between these two activities. On the other hand, before continuing with analysis at this more general level, it should also be stressed that the particular constellation of ideas and practices being accounted for here are those encountered in the ethnography. This is then a theory of shopping in North London, not of shopping in general, and it is a theory of that element of shopping called here provisioning rather than of all forms of shopping – but with the corollary that provisioning represents the overwhelming component of shopping as a whole.

I have no doubt that shopping can be and is in many times and places an entirely different phenomenon from that explored here. The arguments I have made for shopping in Trinidad, the only other shopping I have investigated through ethnography, are very different. They reflect many differences in the way Trinidadians have explored the possibilities of modernity, as well as differences in gender and other social parameters (Miller 1994, 1997: 243–301). Elsewhere, in collaboration with others, alternative aspects of shopping from this same North London context have been explored (Miller et al. in press). There is quite sufficient temerity in generalizing something called 'North London', notwithstanding the varied backgrounds of the shoppers and the lack of community. To try and suggest that these conclusions must also apply to shopping in general would be absurd. Similar logics may well apply to other areas but to assert this depends on the comparative study of the cosmologies foundational to shopping elsewhere, and no such studies have as yet been attempted. The linkages that will be drawn therefore are those most pertinent to the development of the cultural context of North London shopping.

Subjects of Devotion

The subjects of devotion in sacrifice are usually spirits or deities, and in most religions their image is a lot more person-like than thing-like, although the boundary is none too fixed. In the Judeo-Christian tradition, in particular, the image of God is a very human image, almost the quintessence of a humanity that humans themselves aspire to but cannot reach, but which God inhabits and sustains. In polytheistic religions different deities bring to the fore aspects of humanity as with gods that are warlike, feminine or greedy. This allows for considerable diversity in the conceptualization of the devotional ideal. Warner (1976) has, for example, demonstrated considerable regional and historical variation in images of the Virgin Mary as an object of devotion.

The centrality of sacrifice to the Judeo-Christian tradition may be demonstrated by noting the origins of both religions. Although Judaism has several possible starting points, the strongest claim may probably be made by the moment of the granting of the covenant to Abraham. This act follows directly from the episode called the *Akedah*, in which Abraham is prepared to sacrifice his son Isaac. Most modern commentary focuses upon the courage or faith which would have allowed the father to consider sacrificing his own son. Placed back within its historical context we should perhaps be rather more impressed by the origins of a religion in its refusal to countenance human sacrifice – a practice which was followed by its neighbours at that time. In that context this refusal might well have led to the accusation that it was a religion that lacked faith in being unprepared to commit the ultimate sacrificial rites as compared to those around it. The courage was in being prepared, as a religion, to refuse such sacrifices and therefore distinguish itself. As opposed to its neighbours Judaism was explicitly founded in an act of symbolic substitution.

Christianity has a more definite starting-point and it is one that is the clear symbolic inversion of the origins of Judaism. Where Judaism is founded on the refusal of the father to sacrifice the son, Christianity is founded on precisely the image of a sacrifice of a son by a father. Indeed the image of human sacrifice, in the form of the cross, remains to this day the central defining icon of that religion. While animal sacrifice remains a contemporary practice in other world religions such as Islam and Hinduism it has not been a practice in the Judeo-Christian tradition for nearly two millennia. Within Judaism there is a clear sense of evolution where prayer replaces sacrifice as the medium of communication with the divine, to the extent that major interpreters such as Maimonides virtually dismiss sacrifice as a primitive origin that was eliminated with growing sophistication. Indeed, there may well be a link between an initial foundation in symbolic substitution and the abiding characteristic of later Judaism which has tended towards increasingly abstract genres such as the intellectual analysis of law. By contrast, the greater tendency towards a focus upon sentient images and practices in Christianity (whether ascetic or Rabelaisian) may be related to its foundation in a return to a more literal image of sacrifice.

In Christianity sacrifice has not only remained more to the fore in the image of the cross, but as a metaphor it seems to be far more prevalent a model for appropriate religious behaviour. The ideal of sacrifice and especially the abnegation of self-sacrifice remains close to the dominant ideals of Christian devotional love. Over two thousand years of European history it is likely that the interplay between these various images and ideals of love, devotion and sacrifice will have undergone many changes and permutations. Here we need be concerned only with the rather more modest question as to whether there can be drawn any direct historical links between the underlying cosmological foundation of these ideals in religious practice and that which ends up as the kind of love being practised through mundane shopping in contemporary North London.[46]

Even the more parochial question of the longer-term history of love within England is beset with strongly taken and often strongly opposed positions, such as those of Macfarlane, Shorter and Stone. Macfarlane (1987: 123–43) presents what had been assumed to be a rather modern form of love including the mutual affection of partners outside the determination by either wider kin or the requirements of reproduction. This is argued to be generated by a pattern of English individualism, and in particular individual and alienable rights over property, which ultimately go back to almost prehistoric (or at least early medieval) origins, and which have been much less disturbed by later continental influences than had been thought. By contrast, Stone (1977) and Shorter (1975) prefer a more developmental approach where such modern forms of love only appear in tandem with the distinctive features of modernity and capitalism.

It may be safer therefore to narrow the focus upon a still shorter time period. The key question is whether there is evidence for any transmission of a sense of devotion subsumed within a religious notion of sacrifice and the development of love as the ubiquitous legitimation of devotion within the contemporary family. In very general terms, it is surely no coincidence that the same Romantic movement which brought to the foreground a devotional form of love is one of the several outcomes of the growth of secularization that followed from the Enlightenment. It might be suggested that where secularization removed certain key religious images of devotion, the Romantic movement steps in almost immediately to replace them.

These new objects of devotion are various. One of them is clearly the nation-state replete with its own powerful images of sacrifice (see below). But another and perhaps primary focus is on romantic love. One's partner, potential partner or at least idealized partner becomes the object of devotion and the image of the transcendent that one would willingly give one's life for, but also make rather more mundane sacrifices on behalf of. This is the feminine love that already dominates the ideals of value found in the great tradition of English writers from Jane Austen through to the Brontë sisters.

Campbell (1986) sees this period of transformation as central to the rise of modern consumerism. He documents the precise changes which allowed Calvinist and more general Protestant doctrines to be secularized into cultures of sensibility and the particular idea of romantic love that developed during the eighteenth century. Campbell then goes on to develop a trajectory from Protestant conceptualization of the senses to that of sensual satisfaction and hedonism. Although I don't accept that hedonism lies behind most contemporary provisioning, Campbell's study, which is mainly of discourses about love and pleasure, provides the best guide to the development of the discourse (as opposed to the practice) of modern shopping – where hedonism is the fundamental core. Campbell views this hedonistic desire as the other side to the austerity of accumulation that Weber saw as essential to the development of modern capitalism.

I do not seek to challenge the basic hypothesis that the discourse of hedonistic consumption is a concomitant to the rise of love as a secularization of earlier ideals of devotion. But I believe there is another trajectory leading from the same starting-point which remains more firmly within the confines of love as devotion. This leads not merely to love as an element of romanticism, but is equally pertinent to love as the simple devotional duty expected within family life. The key historical moment may be the establishment of modern forms of patriarchy, where that term implies a direct transference of the devotional habitus from a religious setting to a secular setting.

The most complete historical work to directly examine this linkage between religion and family life in England is the study of the rise of the bourgeois ideologies of the eighteenth and nineteenth centuries by Davidoff and Hall (1987). One of the consequences of the gradual impact of secularization may be found in the response taken by religion itself. This included new devotional forms within an evangelical disposition which sought to colonize more directly and completely areas such as family morality (ibid.: 108–9, 113, 114–15, 323, 451). Central to this new domesticity saturated by religiosity is an ideal of the female as wife and mother entirely identified with her devotional duty to her family. The highly gendered nature of this expectation is made evident where the authors note at one point this negative case: 'nevertheless, Evangelical manhood, with its stress on self-sacrifice and influence, came dangerously close to embracing "feminine" qualities' (ibid.: 111).

The implication is that both domesticity and the family are reconfigured in order to create an ideology of gender distinction that comes to dominate the Victorian period and remains highly influential well into the twentieth century. The devotion previously given to the male figure of God shifts to incorporate the male head of the household, with the role of wife becoming that of tending the domestic shrine as a devotional act. Within religious devotion at the time, the clear gendering of Christian worship was seen as a central issue (Gay 1992). With the increasing secularization of the twentieth century the figures of the husband and father shift from mere incorporation through analogy to become themselves the replacement of religious devotion in the cult of the domestic. In short, there is historical evidence that supports a rather literal concept of patriarchy in which men come to appropriate that devotion which was previously directed towards God. If Macfarlane's arguments are followed, this becomes a kind of regression in love from an earlier autonomy and respect for mutual agency.

This might then constitute evidence for a direct transmission of patriarchal devotion into modern forms of love. The source is taken, if not from regimes of animal sacrifice, then at least from the metaphorical image of self-sacrifice as a human obligation (as in Christianity it was once a divine obligation). By the time Schneider (1968) surveys American kinship love becomes almost the sole legitimatory principle behind any kind of relationship outside of the functionalism thought appropriate to work relationships. But even if this trajectory seems plausible for the eighteenth and nineteenth centuries, it does not necessarily follow that it is the source of ideologies and practices observed by Schneider and supported by the current ethnography close to the end of the twentieth century. To make this further connection we have to consider the state of love in a postfeminist age, through attempts to theorize the present state of relationships.

There have been two recent books which attempt to generalize modern love – by Beck and Beck-Gernsheim (1995) and by Giddens (1992) – that are unusual in their keen sense of the contemporary. Both are well aware that they are dealing with a postfeminist dynamic social context, where they emphasize de-traditionalization and individualism. Both stress the rise of the single-person household, the rise in divorce, the sheer diversity of modern household arrangements and the decline in the tight normative structure of nuclear families centred around marriage. In essence, the impact of feminism is held to have created two genders with a new potential for equality. The emphasis in Beck and Beck-Gernsheim is on heterosexual relationships, though, as Giddens (1992: 135–57) shows, there are grounds for seeing homosexual relationships as in some ways at the vanguard of these developments. Within both genders each individual now has powerful normative expectations and cultural pressures to develop themselves as individuals with their own careers, trajectories and what Giddens sees as a project of self-identity.

This leads to the problem of how either of these partners may participate in a relationship which may demand not only considerable compromise but also the subsumption and to a degree the elimination of that same individuality. Both Beck and Beck-Gernsheim and Giddens look to a somewhat brave new world of experimentation and diversity where couples work out a wide variety of possible combinations and arrangements, some of which are successful at least in the sense of 'good enough' forms of relationship. While Beck and Beck-Gernsheim stress experimentation, Giddens is more concerned to model a movement towards a more mature version of what he calls 'confluent love' based on free exchange which thereby exemplifies in the private sphere the kinds of ideals that democracy has for some time represented for the public sphere (1992: 184–204).

These books should be highly relevant to a North London street which fits no one's image of the traditional community but appears to consist just of congeries of isolated households that simply happen to live in juxtaposition. But while these two books may be highly prescient analytical works, they shed relatively little light upon what was ethnographically encountered. One of the underlying assumptions of both books is a drive towards self-expression in relationships where relationships themselves become increasingly subject to explicit dialogue and negotiation. If shopping is an expression of relationships then it should now form part of such an explicit series of negotiations. In practice, however, most shopping is highly routinized and often relates to relationships as a vicarious rather than an expressive medium. It is likely that being able subtly to shift and monitor the nature of kinship and friendship through buying clothes or household goods in many cases substitutes for rather than stimulates explicit dialogue about the relationships themselves.

Furthermore, these authors are sociologists working mainly with relatively abstract accounts, and these abstractions may be misleading. This can be seen when we juxtapose the statistics of change with the ethnographic impression of the street. The statistics which are stressed in their work are ones that show a sharp increase in single-person households, especially in urban contexts. Beck and Beck-Gernsheim (1995: 15) note that in some German towns the majority of households are now single-person. Their theoretical premiss is sustained not only by such statistics but also by sociological work on individualism and de-traditionalization. From such generalizations these authors identify a new world that has to be explained.

As already noted, the presence of single-person households in the ethnographic area is dominated by two main types. The first is that of the elderly who are alone, most often by reason of the death of a spouse and a lack of desire on either side to live with their children. The numbers of these households has grown considerably in the population, though they are mainly present locally as highly impoverished households within the council estate flats. The second type is related to the particular fraction of the middle class that lives in this area. This is dominated by ambitious single females who are attempting to develop careers in areas such as journalism and the media. These individuals certainly exhibit the self-concern and ambition for career that feminism has activated. But when it comes to the everyday mundane world of shopping neither of these type cases should be regarded as either particularly individualistic or de-traditionalized.

The elderly are amongst the most devoted to an orientation to otherness, as has become evident from the analysis of thrift. For a perspective on the single females, the best source of information was a hairdresser whose shop was on this same street and who specialized in this particular market. What was reiterated again and again in conversations within the hairdressing shop was the view that feminism, although achieving considerable advances for these women, has also created a problem in finding suitable partners. At the same time that these women feel they have grown in stature they feel the men of their age have if anything shrunk into relative immaturity and lack of confidence, such that they tend to make very inadequate partners. What does not follow, however, is that these women are either autonomous or looking for autonomy. They still reflect the condition of femininity which Coward (1992) calls 'the desire to be desired'. Their primary ambition, notwithstanding their commitment to a career, is for a satisfactory relationship based on love, ideally with a partner, but if necessary then directed solely at an infant within a single-parent context. Judging from the conversations in this hairdressing context, the search for love could be described as obsessional, far outweighing all other considerations.

There is a post-teenage period of relative autonomy and there are of course exceptions who retain their individualism, but for most of these women as their careers develop, love returns as almost the sole arbiter of happiness or despair. As such, their provisioning is almost always with an eye to the imagination and the potential of an other. In the meantime the act of shopping as provisioning is used by them to refuse rather than maintain individualism. By experiencing their daily shopping as the provisioning of a household, and only separating themselves out as recipients for special 'treats', they can use this normative structure of shopping to reconstitute themselves as a variant of the household, rather than as an individual. Shopping is directed to the household itself that simply happens, for the moment, to have only one person in it. One should be cautious therefore in assuming that being on one's own can be used as statistical evidence for individualism. It is likely that single males have more difficulty in making this daily labour of mundane provisioning the basis for a sense of living within the routines of a household which thereby transcends the individualized self as the recipient of this labour. But my evidence for single men was too sparse for me to generalize.

There may well be regional differences. There are good historical and sociological reasons for expecting that North American shopping may be far more individualistic than North London, though accounts such as DeVault suggest otherwise. Gender relations are not likely to be the same in Scandinavia or Japan. But on a North London street there remains a deeply conservative actuality with a strong emphasis on gender difference underlying a dominant desire for key relationships that continue to be the thing that makes life worth living or at least bearing. This incorporates an ideal in which individuality is given up for devotional care and responsibility. There are now abundant qualitative studies of domestic life by feminist researchers that provide further evidence for this assertion and for seeing confluent love as still largely restricted to particular groups, such as academics, where self-consciousness about relationships is at a premium.

Notwithstanding this caution, a considerable merit of these studies by Beck and Beck-Gernsheim and by Giddens is that, unlike most studies which focus upon the discourse of love, they are concerned with love as contemporary practice. As a practice, the love encountered ethnographically in North London[47] is a relationship that exists within a complex structure of obligation, uncertainty, ambivalence and anxiety. It is love that incorporates its own negatives. For all the foregrounding of love in romanticism, when it comes to everyday life it is often also hidden, fearful and almost embarrassed by itself when it comes to the public life of the private sphere.

Before considering new forms of love as practice, these questions may be returned for the moment to some general discourses on love succinctly discussed in a short paper by Lindholm (1995). Summarizing the literature on love, he argues that there have been two quite different traditions. The first tends to emphasize questions of assessment, interests and alliance as the foundation for acceptable relationships. One of the important points that arises from this literature is that such a view is by no means confined to some postmodern de-traditionalization. It is central to discussions by writers such as Plato, Ovid and most anthropological students of alliance. Such an approach is reactivated by most feminist critiques of domestic relationships with their emphasis upon equivalence as the foundation for justice in relationships.

But there exists a powerful alternative to this 'eros' approach. This is the idea of 'agapic' love, based on adulation which being transcendent is not based on appraisal but rather on the totalizing of otherness. This is a love that is not subject to reason but is unqualified. The aim of such love is precisely the loss of the self through the merging with a beloved other; 'it is above all a creative act of the human imagination, arising as a cultural expression of the deep existential longings for an escape from the prison of the self' (ibid.: 57). Lindholm links this closely with religious devotion, though his main illustration comes from his research on charisma.

Notwithstanding the complexities and ambiguities of love as an expression of partnership in contemporary North London, agapic love still has a commanding presence within the modern practice of love, and remains a key rival to forms of postfeminist love discussed by contemporary sociologists. Belk and Coon (1993) have recently argued for the importance of agapic love through a study of the gifts given during dating and courtship. But there exists a more sustained and in some ways totalizing image of the sheer subsumption of the individual within devotional relationships, that is exemplified in postfeminist parenting. This was clearly evident from the ethnographic material.

The Devoted Mother

Beck and Beck-Gernsheim (1995) are particularly helpful in accounting for one of the key findings of my own research, which is the rise of the infant as a substitute for the partner as the object of contemporary devotion. The degree of concern with infants became evident from the sheer weight of emphasis amongst middle-class mothers upon the infant as a recipient of their shopping. This formed part of an obsessional concern with what foods, clothing and other materials infants should be allowed to consume or be prevented from consuming. The ideal consumption pattern of the infant was closely embedded in a concept of nature which implied that everything that the infant does, whether crying or developing its own rhythm of sleep (and, more to the point, sleeplessness) is an expression of its naturalness and should not be interfered with. This can only be achieved at the expense of the mother.[48] Work is given up, sleep is given up, virtually any independent existence is given up, in the desire not to interfere with 'nature'. Any alteration to the natural rhythm is viewed as a kind of 'intervention', which is the term used for formal medical practices that are seen as the enemy to be avoided during natural childbirth. The breast is never to be refused and any punishment of the child or loss of temper by the mother is the occasion of considerable anxiety and guilt.

Underlying this pattern seems to be the use of consumption to assert a continuity between mother and infant that retains the quality of a biological link between these two. For example, there is a constant emphasis upon breast-feeding as against the use of substitutes. This is followed by a stress upon natural foods and an abhorrence of foods that include artificial ingredients or, in particular, sugar, such as sweets and biscuits. There then develops a series of battles between mother and infant in which eventually the infant gains access to that which had been at first so stridently resisted. This may involve sweets and later other foods such as hamburgers, but also Barbie dolls, toy guns and a wide range of other commodities. In general, they represent in extreme form many of the concerns with the relationship between shopping and love that were the subject of the first chapter.

In a paper which focuses upon this phenomenon (Miller forthcoming, see also Parker 1996), I have argued that there is a common structure to this series of defeats of the mother as the infant gains access to forbidden and feared commodities. As the child develops, the mother's enemy is held to be materialism, in the form of anything from television advertisements to indulgent relatives which would seduce the child into independent desires that cannot be fulfilled by the mother. As such, materialism itself becomes the instrument by which the child develops its autonomy in the teeth of any narcissistic attempt to retain the infant as the mere continuation of the identity of its parents.

For present purposes, what is most striking is that this description fits only one particular group within the diversity of households found in the street. This group may be defined by its membership of the National Childbirth Trust and consists exclusively of middle-class mothers. A common feature of all its members is that they closely identify with the impact of feminism and feminist ideology. The striking paradox is that it was precisely those women who had become most assertive about the centrality of career and autonomous self-development for women, who appeared to be most obsessed by the complete repudiation of these same ideals when reborn as mothers and who become entirely devoted to the needs and whims of their infants. There is another consequence of the emphasis upon the biological linkage between themselves and their infants enhanced by natural childbirth and natural breast-feeding. This has the effect of negating the critique of essentialist conceptualizations of gender that is foundational to feminism, since it reinforces that aspect of mothering which pertains to gender as biological difference.

The suddenness in the change of perspective and direction that occurs when these women are reborn as mothers is itself astonishing. The assertiveness with which they had insisted upon an independent life, refusing the idea that this should be in any way subservient to a male figure, is replaced by an equal assertiveness that they cannot go out and enjoy themselves, sometimes for a year or more, after the birth of the child. Nothing of their own desires should interfere with their obsessions about the proper way to bring up their infants. Historically, this also represents an extraordinarily abrupt shift in the dominant attitudes to childcare. In the first half of this century, the middle-class relationship to the infant was more likely to be dominated by precisely the opposite attitude, summarized as the fear of 'spoiling' the infant.

It was generally held that the erection of barriers to the child's will was good in and of itself since it aided in the task of civilizing the animalistic tendencies of the natural infant, and helped the mother to cultivate a socially acceptable and accepting child. The indulged child would inevitably result in a monster unleashed onto society by the irresponsible mother.

It is surely no coincidence that this complete reversal in the ideology of childcare has been accompanied by the equally sudden emergence of feminism and the removal of what up to that time had been the main taken-for-granted subject of devotion, that is the 'head' of the household. Deeper still lies a trajectory in the development of an obsessional concern with the child as emblematic of human interiority more generally, a point made with some force by Steedman (1995). It seems then that just as thoroughly as secularization pushed the divine off a pedestal as the subject of worship and replaced it with the husband in patriarchy, so feminism has rendered the male partner as an increasingly unworthy subject of devotion. But instead of this resulting in the end of the self-sacrificial model of devotional duty, the husband has been replaced by the newest subject of devotion – the infant.

At the moment of birth is found an exemplary instance of pure agapic love, in the complete subsumption of the individual in another, only tempered by a narcissistic undertone in that the infant is understood as a biological extension and in some sense rebirth of the mother. What seems quite clear is that this does not follow the kind of evolution of love that has been described in postfeminist contexts by Giddens or by Beck and Beck-Gernsheim. There is no negotiation, no compromise, no retention of autonomy. On the contrary, the infant is totally encompassed by the sheer devotional intensity that bears down upon it. It thereby demonstrates that within what might be called ultra-modern contexts, the form of devotion seen in earlier periods within religion or romantic passion is still very much an option.

This finding provides the basis for a conclusion to the consideration of subjects of devotion. Few of us who were brought up at the time when feminism first arrived on the university campus as the white heat of critique would have predicted just how little might have changed over the next two decades when it comes to what was a core concern of feminism: the logic of ordinary domestic practice, that is who does what in the home. Of course, feminism itself is not entirely new. In the mid-nineteenth century the possibilities of radical gender equality were very evident in the work of writers as diverse as Ibsen and Engels. Why should such high and ideal hopes have seen so little in the way of realization? One reason for this evident conservatism in practice may be that what is at issue here goes beyond the simple relationship of females to males in our society. Having been much influenced by Strathern's (1988) anthropological studies in Melanesia, I prefer to take gender ideology as a whole, with the separate genders understood as both generated out of the same ideological developments. In other words, the structure of the relationship between the genders is one that is not specific to that relationship; it may pertain equally to a relationship between humanity and God or between parents and children.[49]

If the 'habitus' that underlies the desire for sacrifice is so powerful that the main response to the critique of each subject of devotion is to find an alternative subject, then perhaps there is some justification for an attempt to elucidate the structure itself. A theory is required that does not reduce structure to its particular manifestations, and the relationships and interest groups that are served by it.[50] Behind these may be discerned a more fundamental, historical and slower-moving development in cosmology that continues to search for its objectification in whatever relationships can be used for that process, rather than being tied to the rise and fall of one particular symbolic opposition such as that of gender. In that sense, love is not more superficial, but if anything rather more basic an issue than that of gender. At this level also, the relationship between sacrifice and shopping becomes not merely one of analogy, but one of continuity of love through discontinuity in the objects of love's devotion to which I now turn.

Objects of Devotion

In turning from the subjects of devotion to the objects of devotion we encounter a common academic and colloquial prejudice

– one that remains responsible for the denigration of shopping and for an unwillingness to see it as a practice that reveals profound rather than trivial developments in human values and beliefs. This is the generic accusation of fetishism that assumes that any emphasis upon material culture *per se* will necessarily take the place of social relations rather than be the means for enhancing social values. At least since the time of Marx's commentaries upon Feuerbach (e.g. 1975: 243–4), a clear parallel has been drawn between this accusation against the commodity as false consciousness and the secular critique of religion as misplaced devotion to objects and images. This accusation is most resolutely laid against the kinds of commodities purchased from supermarkets and chain stores that form the basis for the ethnography of shopping.

In the first part of this essay the argument was made that shopping was largely about social relationships. But even when this is granted there may be resistance to the idea that there can be values created through the range and form of the commodities themselves which contribute to (rather than vicariously take away from) the humanity of the shoppers. This section of the essay will therefore begin with an anthropological account where objects can more readily be granted this status of authenticity. It will end by attempting to develop a parallel argument with respect to the apparently much more trivial contents of the supermarket. It is an essential component of the argument that objects are the means for creating the relationships of love between subjects rather than some kind of materialistic dead end which takes devotion away from its proper subject – other persons.

Weiner – It's Love that Stops the World Going Round

Through his work on sacrifice, Mauss helps to prevent the overextension of what became his own concept of 'the gift', since the relationship created by sacrifice cannot be reduced to one of exchange or reciprocity, let alone that of equivalence. The purpose of sacrifice is precisely to demonstrate the non-equivalence of the sacred and the profane. In a similar fashion, the anthropologist Weiner's (1992) account of inalienable objects is explicitly rendered into an opposition to a trend initiated by Lévi-Strauss and developed by others who, she argues, have over-extended the model of the 'the gift' and of reciprocal exchange into some kind of general principle constitutive of society. This is aimed in part at studies which emphasized the use of both women and sexuality as objects of exchange.[51]

This argument about gender as objectification is linked by Weiner to a larger discussion of the role of objects within processes of objectification. Weiner's concept of inalienable possessions must take its meaning from the contrast to the alienable, that which may be given away, or also that which may be spent or consumed. Weiner (in a similar manner to Bataille) sees her project as part critique and part extension of Mauss and subsequent discussions of the gift. Her study starts from the observation that in many societies there exists a range of objects that are not intended to be given away in exchange, that must be retained rather than entered into the practice of reciprocal exchange. Such objects are often the most powerful symbols of the particular group concerned and of its constancy and stability. It is these object's potential for negating exchange (or one might add expenditure) that turns them into sites for the objectification of transcendence. In their devotion to these objects people objectify their ideal of stable identity, in the sense that the objects come to constitute the materiality of social identity. Much of her evidence is drawn from the Pacific region and the objects concerned are typically items such as valuable cloth or stone adzes.

Although in her first chapter Weiner (ibid.: 40–1) considers Bataille as a significant theorist of exchange, she merely notes his mistaken interpretation of the potlatch. She does not take his stress upon consumption as particularly significant. By taking this perspective, however, one can create a link between her work and the issue of sacrifice. Furthermore, the importance of the inalienable possession becomes its negation of the idea of consumption as expenditure as much as that of exchange. Although these are not sacrificial practices, Weiner makes clear that in many cases people do sacrifice themselves for such objects. Inalienable objects are, as it were, just the kind of things that people fight over and die for. They are symbolic forms that are often constitutive of larger social groups.

It is easy to envisage a trajectory from these emblematic objects of the Pacific to nationalism and the sacred symbols of nationhood which have increasingly become the main altar upon which young lives have been sacrificed over the last two centuries. This violence through which people and possessions are consumed is reflective of that first stage of sacrifice, which so exercised Bataille. It is not, however, an act of sacrifice in the full sense of Hubert and Mauss. Rowlands has recently argued (forthcoming) that such victims of nationalistic war can be transformed *post hoc* into sacrificial rites by creating new inalienable objects such as war memorials which then reconstitute war as the voluntary giving of blood on behalf of a nation which is thereby redeemed. It is the memorial as inalienable object that then transforms a past war into a rite of sacrifice. Memorials, as with land, or nation, or other forms of inalienable object become the objectification of what are purported to be permanent values that transcend and subsume events recast as sacrifices which thereby further ennoble and maintain these images. The more blood that has been shed on their behalf the more sacred they become.

Although Weiner does not speak explicitly of love any more than does the literature on sacrifice, we are clearly dealing with the topic of devotion. Though the emotional context is not abstracted as an affective dimension, there are many instances in the accounts given where affectivity in the form of passion is at least implied, whether this is the Maori fighting over *toanga* or the Pintupi's devotion to original *tjurunga*[52] (ibid.: 61, 108). What emerges clearly is that it is exchange, not love, that as it were 'makes the world go round'. Love, by contrast, tends to act as the very negation of this sense of movement, by confirming a stable and constant centre to one's affective identity.

Weiner's interest is in locating objects regarded within a given cultural logic as inalienable, which may be manufactured or based on the classification of natural forms such as the land. The dominant search for inalienable possessions stems from the philosopher Locke (1970; see also Ryan 1982: 29–48), who developed a similar concern with the legitimation of property, based on the idea of an intrinsic link between people and the results of their productive labour. This argument is in turn bequeathed to Marx, whose central principle behind the concept of value is the same ideal of inalienability. For Marx, while it is clear that commodities under capitalism are alienable, this is understood as in part a denial of an intrinsic inalienability in that they should continue to express the species being of labour. This concern recycled back through Mauss (1966) as the *Hau*, the cosmological principle that the Maori use to define the inalienable element in the gift that creates reciprocity.

My argument is intended to leave behind these rather mystical principles and return to a world where the inalienable is deemed to exist only in as much as a given cultural tradition constructs relationships of material culture in that way. On a North London street there is very little left of a sense of the intrinsically inalienable. Instead, as I have argued elsewhere (Miller 1987), the sense of the inalienability is produced primarily through consumption and the ability of consumption as a process to extract items from the market and make them personal. In North London then, inalienability is not a pre-given property of certain objects because of a prior relationship to some other process such as productive labour. Instead, the inalienable is a rather more fragile property of objects that may hark back to the labour that has produced the money that allows one to possess them, but is increasingly dependent upon the more active labour of consumption that creates a symbolic link to the owner or the relationships involved in their acquisition.

This argument depends upon a particular theory of consumption (Miller 1987). In brief the theory suggests that we confront most objects as highly alienable symbols of either the market or the state. It is the process of consumption itself which through various forms of appropriation such as purchase, time of possession, use and the accretion of particular associations transforms some objects into comparatively inalienable possessions. This is not simply achieved, however. It is based on a splitting of expenditure into two elements. One of these passes through the commodity to the individual as in the case of possessions such as items of clothing or jewellery which over time become highly personal symbols of the self. The other trajectory of consumption remains closer to the argument of Weiner in that consumption becomes part of the objectification of larger social units within which the self is subsumed. An example of this which has already featured prominently within this theory of shopping is the relationship between thrift and the domestic sphere.

Thrift and the House

Thrift has been found to represent the central ritual in the transformation of shopping from spending to saving. This has already opened up the question as to who or what this thrift is directed to. The most sustained attempt by an anthropologist to examine a case study of thrift and answer this same question is a book by Gudeman and Rivera (1990) which takes what may be the quintessential case of thrift, that of the peasant household. Although their case study is set in rural Colombia, their book is particularly useful since they do not take their ethnographic region in isolation but direct a 'conversation' between their South American peasant community and the history of the concept of thrift in classical writing on political economy. Thrift is found to be central to what they call 'the house model'. This exists where the house is the basic metaphor for economic activities. The peasant, for example, works for the house, saves the house's resources and seeks to augment the house. The house in most peasant societies is an example of Weiner's inalienable possessions in that property cannot be sold by an individual – which is the reason why Macfarlane argued England was not a peasant society.

Gudeman and Rivera (ibid.: 166–78) argue that the concept of thrift, as central to efficient household management, is found as a primary objective of 'economic life' in the writings of classical authors of both Greece and Rome, continues in medieval times and remains a dominant concern for authors such as Adam Smith. The latter is quoted as saying: 'capitals are increased by parsimony, and diminished by prodigality and misconduct. Whatever a person saves from his revenue he adds to his capital . . . Parsimony, and not industry is the immediate cause of the increase of capital' (from Smith 1976 [1776]: 358–9). Smith did, however, depart from the peasant logic in assuming that money saved is ultimately spent rather than hoarded. This led eventually to the full rebuttal of such concerns with Keynes, who saw the interest paid on savings as the reward for risk-taking investment as opposed to hoarding.

Gudeman and Rivera use this sequence to oppose the logic of the peasant household to the workings of the capitalist firm with its primary concern for making profits. Most explicitly they contrast the house model with the 'body' model of the corporation. Under the capitalist corporation the drive is the reinvestment of savings for the furtherance of profits, minimizing storage and maximizing exchange, eschewing the larger moral and kin-based imperatives of the home and reducing legitimation to profit-making. Unfortunately, while this dichotomy between the corporation and the peasant house as productive units is clearly important, at no point do Gudeman and Rivera make the other obvious comparison which would be between the peasant house and the household under capitalism as units of consumption. If they had done so, our understanding of the consequences of capitalism might be very different.

While Gudeman and Rivera concentrate on the centrality of the house to the self-understanding of economic relations, the house clearly represents much more than this. Their work demonstrates that the house works as a metaphor for kindred, and this is found in many societies where the very concept of lineage is encapsulated within the house. The house may be metaphor, but as with many metaphors it thereby helps constitute something which cannot easily be objectified, in this case a sense of transcendent identity to which individuals belong and devote their lives, or, as in the case of Romeo and Juliet, flout at their peril. This cosmological potential of the house is precisely the problem raised by a recent collection edited by Carsten and Hugh-Jones (1995) and called *About the House*. This begins with some speculation by Lévi-Strauss implying that there may be a category which transcends the concept of kinship as a relationship between persons, and owes something to, but is equally not reducible to, the house as material culture.[53]

There is a clear parallel between the various essays on the house in Carsten and Hugh-Jones and a well-established debate about the nature of the 'household'.[54] This also centres on the problem constituted by the household being neither quite a category of domestic kinship, nor reducible to the mere spatial juxtaposition of living together. Rather the term 'household' feeds off and exploits the ambiguity between these two realms of classification. Carsten and Hugh-Jones show very clearly that the house (and one could add the household) thereby plays a key role in cosmology, in the way people relate to concepts of what transcends them as individuals, and what in the tradition of Lévi-Strauss, might be called symbolic power. In conclusion, they wish to see the house as a kind of symbolic process which carries people through life as the focus of their identity and as perhaps the core inalienable possession. The examples used in Carsten and Hugh-Jones are all taken from what are commonly called tribal societies, but by including the concept of household the extension to non-tribal societies is made explicit.

The pity is that Carsten and Hugh-Jones, while acknowledging Gudeman and Rivera, fail to exploit the latter's key finding, which is that in everyday life the main means by which the house works as just such a process is through the practice of thrift. In turn, Gudeman and Rivera, with their focus upon political economy, do not develop the cosmological implications of their research into the centrality of thrift. In shifting from the tribal and peasant contexts to that of North London, a rapprochement between these two perspectives on the house is required. In North London, while the house is certainly an important part of identity, it is no longer a key metaphor for lineage and inter-generational descent. Nor does it retain the core metaphorical role given in 'the house' model. People do not use the term 'house' or seem to think of their house in this way. I would argue that it is thrift which has remained to become the primary means by which a concept of house, in the sense used by these studies, is retained. This is part of a general argument that thrift has thereby moved from being largely a means to an end, to becoming an end in itself. This observation is, however, quite compatible with both of these books because of their stress on the house as a process, rather than as a fixed entity. If thrift is the means by which the process is in effect carried out, then it can easily be understood to have the potential for becoming in and of itself the primary means by which that process is maintained.

To make this clearer, it is worth reflecting briefly on the trajectory that leads historically towards the kind of thrift that is observed in the ethnography. There has been a considerable amount of recent historical work on the development of the modern household in England. Historical studies of the eighteenth and nineteenth centuries suggest a gradual but inexorable rise of the bourgeois and middle-class household as against the aristocratic household,[55] and that a key feature of the bourgeois household is a thrift so carefully monitored and controlled as to appear very close indeed to the situation of the peasant household. Vickery (1993) provides an exemplary case study of the centrality of thrift to one household manager in late eighteenth-century England. These studies demonstrate that, as in the case of the peasant house, household management becomes the means to preserve and stabilize a goal in life, almost irrespective of the behaviour of the members of the household that are supposed to constitute the home.

Although Frykman and Lofgren (1987: 28), amongst others, try to claim that bourgeois thrift is quite different from peasant thrift in Sweden, I see little evidence to support them. Furthermore, recent work on working-class households in nineteenth-century Britain show an equal concern to use thrift in order to differentiate themselves as respectable, with thrift clearly demarcated as a moral rather than simply a functional concern even amongst the poor. It is thrift which enables them to separate themselves from those seen as sunken into moral degeneracy owing to an inability to control expenditure. Domestic thrift as an expression of self-respect rather than of the social sharing of expenditure thereby became the dominant character of working-class households (Benson 1994: 210–11, Daunton 1983, Pahl and Wallace 1988). Contemporary and further historical work on the divisions of labour by Pahl (1984) also suggests this continuity in the domestic as a moral unit within which thrift plays a central role, for working-class as much as middle-class families. I think we are safest to assume, along with Pahl and Wallace, that 'domesticity', then, is not a value born of contemporary consumption 'but has been an essential element in working-class life for as long as we have any historical knowledge of the context and nature of everyday life' (1988: 141). Taken together, these studies become evidence for considerable continuities in the long-term development of modern thrift.

I have argued elsewhere (Miller 1995, 1997) that this centrality of thrift has tremendous consequences for the political economy. Most of the 'new right' economics is based on the goal of savings on price for the consumer. In Britain, Margaret Thatcher's most common source of legitimation was to appeal to the idea of the natural thrift of a housewife, which she claimed to understand as the daughter of a grocer. At one level the whole of GATT and the market economy is based on the idea that it facilitates the consumers of the world in saving money. So consumer thrift is now the centrepiece of global economic ideology, with all the consequential deleterious effects upon the producers of the developing world. The irony has become that the major legitimation for the continuity of suffering for producers has become the morality of consumers. This is itself a complex set of relationships, which will not be discussed here since the present essay deals only with the local causes and consequences of thrift.

When we turn back to the ethnography of shopping, the problem with understanding the significance of thrift is that it is too easily accounted for by simple explanations. There is the temptation to apply Occam's razor and dismiss it as quite obvious activity. The meaning of thrift is not, however, universal. In some times and places thrift is clearly a simple expression of poverty. For shoppers in Trinidad (Miller 1997: 274–6) of equal importance would be the rivalry between female relatives wanting to demonstrate their skills by buying the same goods cheaper than someone else. Thrift in that context was primarily about competition between members of extended families. Within the London ethnography the most common understanding of thrift was in relation to skill or in answers to questions about whether shopping was a skill. But there is considerable evidence within the ethnography to suggest that thrift as expressed in shopping is all these things but also much more than any of them. The evidence suggests that thrift also has to be understood as an extension of those larger concerns that are evident in the general literature on inalienable possessions, the house and the objectification of value.

This is suggested by the lack of any relation between the importance of thrift and the levels of income or resources. As shown in the ethnographic section, wealthy households buying expensive goods are just as able to translate their shopping into a form of thrift as poor households buying the cheapest goods. The historical traditions behind bourgeois thrift are just as powerful as those behind the thrift of the respectable working class. Second, there seems very little evidence to suggest that in most cases thrift is actually a means to save money. In many cases it is equally the justification for spending more money. The supermarket 'saver' proved to be by far the most important reason why shoppers bought groceries that they had not intended to buy or did not feature on their shopping lists. Several shoppers saw thrift shops, car boot sales and the like as key sites of later regretted expenditure. For many, the sales were the key time of considerable spending. There were other occasions when thrift clearly does save money for careful shoppers who 'shop around' and are willing and able in effect to trade time for money. So thrift can neither be explained simply as a form of spending or of saving. Finally, and most important, was the evidence for the sheer ubiquity of thrift. When considered within this larger historical and comparative context it may be less surprising that thrift might come to occupy its present central role in the ritual transformation of shopping from the fantasy of spending to the fantasy of saving money. This leads back to a conclusion that thrift has come to supplant the house itself as the process by which economic activity is used to create a moral framework for the construction of value.

The Material Culture of Love

If the analysis of thrift as cosmology helps us to understand why people make a ritual of saving out of the act of shopping, then we need a complementary answer to the question as to why and how people spend. Thrift and saving constitute the second stage of the rite of sacrifice/shopping during which a sense of household as transcendent object of devotion is created. In the third stage the emphasis shifts to the family or its substitutes as the particular recipients of goods. This returns us to the profane world of consumption as spending. Consumption is often argued to be about choice, and in particular free choice amongst endless opportunities of difference. In practice, however, the largest measure of our consumption is not derived from a desire for more things or for more choice. It comes from the gradual expansion of a sense of what ordinary people may ordinarily expect as their standard of living combined with the growth in their incomes. Whether it is the speed with which a medical operation should be carried out, or the number of toilets in a family house, modern consumption has certainly demonstrated how hard it is to overestimate our capacity to need as opposed merely to want. Shoppers have not the slightest problem in constantly bemoaning what they perceive as a lack of choice for a particular commodity while standing in the middle of a shopping mall.

Choice has a very limited role in the theory of shopping outlined here. The love that is the main force which carries provisioning through is rarely much to do with choice except in the initial stages of courtship between partners. The love described here has much more to do with obligation, duty and a set of predispositions which exist prior to the relationship which manifests them. It is situated largely within the expectations of kinship and pattern of interdependence that Finch (1989; see also Allan 1996) has mapped in terms of the changing dynamics of the family in contemporary Britain. These studies demonstrate the limited role of choice in family relationships and this is in turn reflected in the limited role of choice when studying the way commodities are used as part of the technology of love within the family.

In asking why people spend, there exists an opposition between economics, consumer behaviour and psychology, all of which tend towards the emulation of science and models of universals, and the more qualitative and relativist tradition in anthropology, geography, history and sociology.[56] In recent times qualitative studies have increasingly acknowledged the possible autonomy of consumption from production. There is no longer much support for the idea that we are merely the passive recipients of whatever capitalism produces. There is too much evidence to suggest that most attempts to sell us goods fail. Desire is at the least discriminatory and often unpredicted by commerce.[57] Capitalism plays its role in the construction of desire but it is by no means the sole determinant of where and when values and relationships become subject to commodification. This is perhaps easiest to see when commoditization is most abrupt and intrusive. Through a historical study of the use of soaps and toiletries in Zimbabwe, Burke (1996) shows how soap comes to be inscribed as a necessity through a sustained campaign of commercial sales and ideological pressures. Yet at the same time a series of other products such as margarine come to have equal status as necessary commodities for use within an already existing cultural tradition of smearing the body, without any noticeable commercial pressure to create the commodification of this tradition.

Instead, qualitative studies have recently focused upon the relationship between identity and consumption, though historians have shown that the genres of identity which may be objectified in commodities are neither given nor stable. Auslander (1996), for example, has plotted the way women in nineteenth-century France found a succession of domains which they were expected and encouraged to represent through commodities, that is the family, class, the nation and finally the self. Sennett (1976), looking to the longer term, traced a shift from a time (during the *ancien régime*) when social identity was inscribed in the outer appearance of persons in public space, to an increasing orientation to a subjectively controlled interiority where the true self was to be located, but which still had to find expression through external appearance. Thanks to such detailed historical studies it has become clear that the aspects of social identity that commodities pertain to are not fixed or immutable, but have shifted as the conceptualization of identity has itself changed.

In developing theories as to the nature of consumption the anthropologists of the 1970s tended to concentrate on the social construction of categories, most especially social categories, as providing fields for the play of commodities as material culture. Douglas and Isherwood (1978), working within the paradigm of semiotics, saw commodities as a system for communication which makes visible and stable the categories of culture, with an emphasis upon social difference, exclusion and inclusion. Others such as Baudrillard (1981; also Sahlins 1976) attempted a semiotic mapping in which objects come to represent specific social positions. The fullest exposition of this particular anthropological perspective was given by Bourdieu (1984) in his analysis of taste, where it was the classification of class position that was deemed fundamental. As already noted, the ethnography that forms the basis of this essay has been used elsewhere (Miller et al. in press, ch. 7) to demonstrate the continued importance of class identity for these same shoppers.

The effect of all these studies, however, if we remain within this mapping onto social space is to make our understanding of consumption rather too mechanical as in the following quote which suggests consumption arises from 'the history of social space as a whole, which determines tastes by the intermediary of the properties inscribed in a position, and notably through the social conditionings associated with particular material conditions of existence and a particular rank in the social structure' (Bourdieu 1996: 256). Such approaches all focus upon a relationship between an individual and a larger context understood as 'society' or a social space, within which the possibilities for individual expression may derive their meaning and potential.

Their source for such theories has often been literary. Sennett makes considerable use of the way novelists explored these relationships. Balzac, in particular, is held to have been examining the development of an expression of character through clothing that can be transmitted by the discerning author and read by the discerning reader. Balzac certainly provides many examples of a rich description of subjects through their associated objects, but these tend to be relatively static portraits, the literary equivalents of the still life in painting, where character and even morality can be communicated through such juxtapositions (see Schama 1993). Douglas and Isherwood's (1979: ix–xii) most sustained example comes in the preface to their book, through extracts from the novels of Henry James, who provides a more dynamic form of character representation and development, but one still tied to social role and position.

These novelists tend to concentrate on possessions – on given accoutrements, that frame the construction of particular persons and personalities. But shopping is not about possessions *per se*, nor is it to be about identity *per se*. It is about obtaining goods, or imagining the possession and use of goods. Many of the goods obtained are consumed in the short term: foods eaten, cosmetics and toiletries used up, many toys and clothes once given hardly used at all. The result is not just stable things that can stand for stable people or for character. The very transitory nature of shopping helps us to comprehend it as a mode of objectification in the Hegelian sense, that is a dialectical process of creation which cannot be reduced to either subject or object. A social relation is not often a 'thing', to be stood for.[58] The bulk of provisioning is related to a state in an ongoing relationship, an underlying constancy complemented by a mood, a compromise, a smile, a punishment, a gesture, a comfort, all the minutiae that make up the constantly changing nuances of a social relationship.

I would not pick Balzac or Henry James to exemplify consumption. They remain too close to the still life or portrait. My preference would be for those modern novelists (Anne Tyler comes to mind) who strive to follow relationships through their expression in everyday worlds. The shopper is not building up a portrait through layers of images, but rather moving in tandem with the changing context. One choice compensates for the last, and provides grounds for shifting towards the next. The material culture of shopping works with complex temporal structures of change, stability and the daily developments in any given relationship. It is closer to those anthropological reports of hunter-gatherer societies in which people moved camp each day in part so they could shift the position of their hut to reflect (but also to affect) the current state of their relationship to particular kindred. For this task we need to consider the very different possibilities given by the diversity of goods.

It is possible to account for a considerable range of the current commodity forms and genres within modern capitalism in terms of the complexity of the relationship between persons in a household. For example, from the point of view of commerce a key (and highly bankable) asset is the long-term brand, that is a specific make of commodity that has existed for generations. An example might be Heinz tomato soup. From the point of view of the family, such brands become appropriated into the desire to constitute the family as a descent group. The notion of a descent group is often infused with a cyclical element, where the role of parent to child returns to the models and guidance that they received from their parents. There are a number of key brands such as Heinz or Kelloggs which are available for objectifying the concept of descent group simply because of their actual longevity as a product and their use in the romantic memorialization of the love that was borne between an earlier generation.

Soup is perhaps a rather obvious example, but it is possible for a brand of toilet roll or kitchen cleaner also to evoke such generational links (usually implicitly), precisely because they become an invariant feature of the grocery purchasing, something that the house as a whole should never run out of. It is not that any one such commodity can bear this weight of descent constitution, but that within many households there is a group of long-standing branded goods which stand for a continuity that transcends any particular generation. So far from consumption standing for change and modernity, the legacy of such brands is that they have remained constant, predictable and little changed during a century which has seen the most immense shifts in social structures and cultural ideology. As such, commodities become the objectification of family tradition, stability and history, which may be one of the reasons that the elderly shoppers seemed particularly conservative with respect to brand choice.[59]

In direct opposition to long-standing brands are fads and fashions whose whole purpose lies in their very transience. A mother who is concerned that her child always has the latest thing so that he or she will not be looked down upon in the playground is expressing her love for and anxiety about that child just as much as when she buys Heinz tomato soup. Of course, the two tendencies may be structurally linked. The latest demand may be for goods linked to *The Hunchback of Notre Dame* or *The Little*

Mermaid, where it is crucial as to which particular week the items are bought. At the same time these refer back nostalgically to *Bambi* and *Snow White*, as the Walt Disney events of her own childhood.

Writers who concentrate on the logic of commerce tend to assume that contradictions in commodity presentation are themselves evidence of the ability of commerce to fool the consumer. Thus Fine and Leopold (1993: 151–2) attack the marketing of dairy goods that literally cream off the fat content in order to provide a wide range of low-fat goods such as milk and yoghurts but then use the same fat to make high-fat cheeses and creamed goods. From the point of view of working with shoppers, however, there is probably nothing better suited to the tasks of shopping than a range of goods which exhibit contradiction. There are very few shoppers who do not use low-fat diet-conscious goods, and it is equally rare that these selfsame shoppers do not also want to buy rich cream desserts that gain their specialness out of direct contrast with the low-fat norm. It is this wide register of fat content that allows the housewife to compose her particular melody of provisioning, whose base notes of healthy diet harmonize with the high notes of treats and rewards. It is the same register that allows her subtly to fatten up the thin little child who never seems hungry while keeping such goods from the problematic larger child who is always raiding the fridge. Indeed, much more subtle notes can be sounded, such as what 'mood' she is in, the need to quickly elicit a smile from a child when a stranger approaches or to conspicuously register her own abstemiousness and depression when a family member is behaving badly. The basket of goods is a composition designed to create harmony and avoid dissonance. (Unless it is dissonance itself that is intended – there are, after all, also modernist shoppers who select for effect.)

To take just one example. Diane is a housewife in a family that exhibits much the same norms as that of Mrs Wynn, in that her husband tends to concentrate on purchases for himself while she buys for the household as a whole. She is currently a full-time housewife in a middle-class environment with children aged two and five. I first met Diane at a Tupperware party, where her choices were specifically of goods that drew a nostalgic response as signifying the Tupperware she remembers her mother using when she was a child. The diversity of goods they require are exploited to make shopping compatible with her husband's sense of autonomy. For example, he buys alcohol for the couple, but at the same time for himself, in that he sees this as his own arena of knowledge and appreciation. As she notes at one point:

A He's more likely to buy beer, probably well different types of beer, yeah, different brands rather than just the cheap French bottles [of wine] which I would get. He'll buy cans of something different.

His choice of more expensive and indulgent goods clearly derives from his role defined against shopping as mundane provisioning. As when asked if his shopping is different from hers:

A Yes definitely, he doesn't cater for the children at all. Not for during the week. For the weekend. He doesn't see their needs during the week – that I've got to provide five teas a week for them and dinners for Patrick and me. So he wouldn't buy anything particularly that would cover that.
Q Other difference?
A He's more likely, I think, to be slightly more frivolous as well. Yes I really try and stick to healthier things and he'll come back with full-fat cheeses and stuff to eat like that.

Similarly, while she buys most of the goods for her children, she approves of a degree of autonomy where the children learn to choose for themselves, often in opposition to her choices. So although she states:

A I would prefer her in shorts and leggings and things like that. She will wear dresses any day of the week. If I let her loose on choosing her own dresses she would come up with, I would think the most awful things, full of ribbons and bows and flounces, which isn't me at all.

In practice she does allow her infant to choose such dresses and feels this is an important skill in developing her own taste.

One of the most common ways to resolve such conflicts is to give children a particular time when they can have more influence, as in the following quotation about breakfast cereals.

A No, she's fairly good. Actually we worked it out that at holidays she can choose whatever she wants, so she can have cocoa pops or variety packs for when it's special holiday time. The rest of the time she just chooses between ricicles – not ricicles – rice crispies or cornflakes, the non sugar-coated ones. Holiday she has free range.

Not everything can be so easily resolved, however.

A She'll try and drag you towards the middle bit of Tesco's now which has got the toys and I try and avoid it so we don't go through it. I try and skirt that bit desperately.

Contradictions develop not only in her expression of her relationships but also in shopping for herself. As with many women, her occasional craving for something new or special, works against a backdrop of a desire to rest or relax into some kind of constancy of appearance that does not require much in the way of active choice. As she notes:

A I suppose what's in the shops I suppose. I never look at women's magazines fashion pages to see what's the latest. I suppose what's in the shops really and what you see on other people I would imagine, and I suppose when you get older there are styles you just tend to stick to anyway and those styles might change slightly with the fashion but you know you know.
Q They're you.
A Yes you're not going to be too . . . like I suppose most people, certainly my generation, will have jeans in their wardrobe somewhere, I don't know, not all generations are the same, but well there was a place when people didn't wear jeans when I was teaching once, not very long but . . .

What emerges overall, from talking to Diane and watching her shop (but equally from talking with and watching so many others), is that when all these complexities of her situation are considered – nostalgia for the old; excitement of the new; responsibility for her relationships; acknowledging their autonomy; moral and financial considerations, and many more such concerns – when one tries to empathetically follow the logics of these internal arguments, then it becomes possible to tease out the specifics of the goods she chooses, why a brand item here and a value label there, why her own taste here and something she loathes there.

There is no need to presume that family relations have somehow become more complex or nuanced as a result of the range of groceries available. Insightful dramas were being written about the tensions and tragedies of kinship as both love and obligation in plenty of other periods and regions. It is merely that this is the core pre-given need which literally feeds off the grocery-store shelf as the range of commodities allows ever more precise and varied objectifications of these same relationships. The key change that allows this multitude of differences to be absorbed is the move from marking relationships as categories to the use of shopping to constitute the present state of the dynamics of a relationship.

This consideration of the objects of devotion began with Weiner's case studies where objects stand clearly for the inalienable. This was itself important in that she thereby demonstrates the possibility that material culture may enhance rather than detract from the capacity to objectify social values. But it is one thing to grant this status to inalienable objects, it is quite another to treat highly alienable commodities in this way. The switch becomes possible when we realize that in North London it is persons, not things, who have become the objectification of the inalienable. As Kopytoff (1986) and my own work (Miller 1987) have suggested, the degree of inalienability of commodities results from the object becoming part of personification through the act of consumption. If persons and relationships become the primary medium through which we achieve a sense of the transcendent or the inalienable, then in turn any objects which express persons or relationships become the vehicle for expressing these higher values. Ironically then, it is the alienable commodity that in our society becomes the mode for realizing, through a process of subjectification, our imagination of the inalienable.[60] The problem in our society is not (as has often been held) that we have become too devoted to objects, but that unlike almost every other society we seem unwilling to allow any mediation in our direct devotion to subjects.[61] Anything that stands between us and a pure subjectivity of the beloved is suspect as a form of fetishism or reification.

The emphasis upon these small-scale social relations and upon the minutiae of difference does not occur in isolation from the wider transformations of modernity. The sense of specificity which is provided for by the details of selection in shopping is directly related to the perception that we live within ever more abstract and vast institutions of production and governance. There has been a marked resistance to attempts to relate social identity to the state (as promoted in socialist societies) or to the market (as promoted in capitalist societies) *per se*. The alienation we feel from such institutions drives the desire to create through consumption itself. Consumption, far from being the continuation of the projects of production and distribution, whether in capitalist or socialist systems, is actually the point of negation, where the particularity of goods is used to create fluid relationships in direct opposition to the vastness of markets and states.[62] So the intricacies of our relationships expressed through consumption reassure us that we are not merely the creatures and categories of capitalism or the state – this is the very opposite of the effect of commodities upon us that we usually assume, when we take goods to be merely symbols of capitalism or the state.

It should also be evident that the dynamic relationship of subjects and objects is not one of representation. The argument is not that goods symbolize persons or identity. Shopping is an active praxis which intervenes and constitutes as well as referring back to relationships. Shopping may, for example, become a vicarious expression of relationships that prevents those involved from being more explicit about what is happening. Family quarrelling becomes an issue about whether individuals are eating their vegetables or 'would be seen dead in that skirt' and not about basic incompatibilities between persons. Shopping may reveal contradictions between self-image and the idealization or denegration of self by others. It may express the nature of power as the coercive gift that cannot be refused or the humble accordance with what has been prescribed by others. Perhaps most fundamental is the sheer routine and unexpressive nature of shopping as a reflection of the sheer routine and unexpressive nature of taken-for-granted relationships. The aim of this essay has been merely to demonstrate that shopping is about relationships, and the consequences of this observation. It leaves to the good novelist the task of demonstrating the profound nature of relationships *per se*.

Conclusion: Shopping and the Dialectic of Subjects and Objects of Devotion

When shopping is understood in terms of the dynamics of social relations there emerges a very simple but fundamental similarity between the act of shopping and the act of sacrifice. The primary purpose of sacrifice when seen from the perspective of the non-believer is an activity that constructs the divine as a desiring subject. The point of smoke rising up to the deity is that it confirms that there exists a deity who wishes to be fed in this manner. The central purpose of shopping is now seen to be precisely the same. Shopping is the construction of the other as the desiring subject. The purpose of shopping is not so much to buy the things people want, but to strive to be in a relationship with subjects that want these things.[63] In both sacrifice and shopping the believer prefers to conceptualize the relationship from the opposite direction, that is that they merely provide for the given wants of their subjects. In either case they may be faced with unwelcome evidence that in the event this was not the case. Hence the despondent reply 'I wish . . .' to the question as to whether the husband makes requests to the housewife who is about to go shopping. If shopping is the siren's song trying to captivate family and friends into becoming the ideal subjects that desire what is given them, then it finds its analogy in the chanted prayer that accompanies sacrifice and whose rhythmic force is intended to entice the deity to partake in the sweet savour of the offering. What the shopper desires above all is for others to want and to appreciate what she brings.

This conclusion implies as its premiss that there should exist within the population a section for whom this process of constructing the other as desiring subjects is central to their cosmology, that is to their understanding of the purpose of this world and their place within it. A core intention of this final chapter was to bring evidence to bear that there exists a 'habitus' – a set of dispositions – that is the foundation to certain people's being ascribed these aspirations as their 'nature'. That is to say, their desire to sacrifice precedes the existence of any subject to that sacrifice. This remains a primary function of the constitution of gender in the contemporary world, and its strength lies precisely in that it is not simply constituted by one historical period or object as, for example, patriarchy. Its roots lie in religious devotion that make it both the prehistory of patriarchy and the posthistory of a cult of the infant that has yet to fully develop, but will emerge as a direct result of the undermining of patriarchy by feminism.

This is consistent with the findings of an ethnographic study in which, even though both genders undertook shopping, shopping as a category was overwhelmingly associated with women.[64] Furthermore, it was women who were predominantly represented by themselves and others as the natural gender of love. Love was found to be the foundational legitimation (the only acceptable grounds) for what in practice is a technology of care and devotion which includes obligation, ambivalence, resentment and the many other negative as well as positive attributes that surround its daily practice. This revolves around an often obsessive concern with the micro-trajectories of a few key relationships to which love can be ascribed.[65]

The ethnographic study focused upon love as the primary context of shopping. It was suggested that this is supported by the weight of feminist work on the domestic sphere, and that the theory presented here remains consistent with these earlier portrayals of the basic inequalities that dominate the domestic sphere. Little has been said about the nature of power implicated in this description. On this issue there seems no reason to dissent from the conclusions of such feminist research. The term 'love' is used because of its centrality to informants' self-understanding, but throughout this essay it has been stated that this is not the romantic ideal of love, but rather love as the ideological foundation for the complex relations that exist between household members.

Love as a practice is fully acknowledged to incorporate coercive pressures. These may involve force where inequality is evident, or ideology where inequality is hidden from consciousness but present as hegemony. This may be experienced as the resistance of husbands and children to dominant housewives attempting to define them through shopping, though this was less commonly observed than that of the female shopper exasperated by the lack of value given to her devotional labour. But while acknowledging that love between spouses and between parents and children commonly incorporates ambivalence to the point of hatred, I have not sought to fully explore this phenomenon. The aim of this essay has been to demonstrate that shopping is primarily about love. It does not pretend to attempt to resolve all the complex questions as to what love itself is about.

Most of the inhabitants of the street appear to live within faith, a faith in love. It may be a rather unsatisfactory, just-about-good-enough-if-you-make-allowances kind of love (or not!). It may be a love that derives as often from the given and negotiated relationships of kinship as the sought relationships of partners and friends, but there is still the relentless mission to pursue or to maintain it. Beyond the immediacy of relationships lies the consequence of a thrift that has shifted from being the means to being the end. For many women, it is they, rather than men, who retain an awareness that there is more to life than just living it, and that the purpose of life lies in its relation to something that transcends it. Shopping so far from being, as it is inevitably portrayed, the essence of ungodliness, becomes as a ritual the vestigial search for a relationship with God.

My theory of shopping not only takes from sacrifice this primary goal of constituting the other as the subject of desire, but argues for a basic homology of ritual structure. The evidence from this chapter suggests that this is more than mere analogy. The first stage within both is a discourse of excess: a vision of transgressive and destructive consumption. This is in turn negated by the second stage, which operationalizes the fundamental habitus of devotion through sending smoke up to the deity or in the transformation of spending into saving. In the third phase, the ritual turns back to the profane relationships of love and social order. Sacrifice or shopping then becomes the ritual mechanism by which these relationships are reconstituted. For shoppers, they are usually highly dynamic relationships re-ordered by the very contingency and specificity of each act of shopping. In the case of sacrifice this is most often the reaffirmation of relationships between people representing fixed categories such as priest or supplicant through the distribution of sanctified food.

Both rituals depend upon the medium of objects, be these commodities or victims. Sacrifice involves the transformation of the objects of consumption from being merely mundanely consumed in profane acts to being transmuted into a higher regime of value where they partake of a relationship which constitutes the divine. Sacrifice thus transforms consumption from being a mere negation of the object in consumption into an act of objectification in the Hegelian sense – that is a form of self-alienation which constructs the dynamic of its own subject. Similarly in shopping, it is through the medium of objects, in this case the very diversity and range of commodities, that the subject is constructed in relation to the shopper. As in the anthropological concept of *The Gift* (Mauss 1966), the object constitutes the relationship, transcending the separate identity of both parties. Commodities have replaced the gift because under modernity a relationship is no longer understood as existing between people as signs of social categories. Rather the ideal is that as characters in a good novel we explore ourselves and develop each other in terms of the potential of the relationship.

The examples taken from Weiner and the literature on 'the house' provide important links between sacrifice and shopping.

In the cases presented by Weiner it is inalienable possessions which constitute society itself as the subject of devotion. In our society, by contrast, inalienable goods can no longer play this role, since both society as transcendent goal and property as reified possession have become condemned as vicarious goals of devotion. Today only human subjects and relationships may stand as inalienable. Objects are therefore judged on their ability to objectify personal and social values and condemned when, as Marx argued of the commodity, they fetishize or in some other way diminish those values. Yet ironically as transience and ambivalence become crucial attributes of relationships it has become primarily commodities that have emerged with the flexibility and abundance to objectify them. Fully alienated through the forces of production and distribution, they become through consumption resaturated with human projects of value creation.

Commodities do not have meaning, in that neither relationships nor identity are a form of language. Rather they are meaningful – they come to matter as means for constituting people that matter. Shopping may be said to evolve from sacrifice in that sacrifice tends to a rather severe taxonomy of social order sanctified by the eating of the sacrificial victim. Shopping, by contrast, is based on an extraordinary range of possible forms and choices, which combine as the many complementary and contradictory elements of a relationship. Love also becomes transformed from unquestioning devotion into a potential for plural and interpretive relationships.[66] This difference between sacrifice and shopping is almost re-enacted in the dynamics of mother–infant relations. Post-feminist mothers often start with a return to pure (self-)sacrifice, agapic love expressed in the extremes of self-denial and abnegation. Over time, however, a distance arises through the increasing need to recognize the autonomy of the infant. As the relationship gradually shifts from total dependence to one of increasing respect through the labour of years of monitoring and sensitive learning, the result if and when it achieves these goals, could genuinely be considered mature. In ideal (though still rare) cases it may become a manifestation of the mutual respect implied by Giddens' (1992) concept of confluent love.

To view this as a progressive tendency is to acknowledge its potential rather than to describe its present form. Love remains central to the preservation of exploitation and inequality in the family. Processes such as parent–infant development may become pathological if one element of this process is removed from the dialectic and taken as a logic in its own right. Love of infants, just as love for partners, can become obsessive and tyrannical. Furthermore, as the example of the infant shows, this debasement does not depend upon external coercion. We can achieve such states of dependency very effectively through acts of projection onto our very own children. Yet even if the focus is turned on to the immense problems of social relations, whether enjoyed through fictive instances such as 'The Simpsons' or confronted as the statistics of children leaving home, the ethnography suggests that love remains the unquestioned legitimacy behind the existence of such relations. If this creates the anxiety as to whether they are failing, the failure does nothing to undermine the ideological centrality of love.

It is not surprising that many academics and popular ideologies tend to lose heart with this maturing of the contradictions of modernity and long for something simpler and pure. There is a restless search for new forms of authentification. In post-structuralist and postmodern angst about superficiality there is a continual search for some way out of equivocation which tends to be regarded as inauthenticity. Many are seduced by ideas such as violence as the immediate constitution of the social. It is also much simpler to dismiss shopping as merely the extrudance of capitalism. The melodies of shopping are constantly denied by a dominant discourse that views this labour of women as mere superficiality and unwarranted desire which, without any of its own creativity or responsibility, merely sings the tunes (or more likely the jingles) that commerce has composed for it.

But the articulation between shopping and capitalism is surprisingly mediated. While capitalism provides the commodities and thrives on the desire by consumers to use them, this is not the reason capitalism exists. Capitalism has its own independent logic of expansion, for which it matters little that goods are consumed within this or that context just as long as they sell. Similarly, the consumer is not merely expressing some spirit of capitalism. The theory proposed here accounts neither for the production nor the distribution of goods. The more important

link was historical. Marx documented for us the relentless destruction by capitalism of an *ancien régime* that gave stability to
social forms. It is the new flexibilities in social relationships that
feed off the potential for goods as a means of expressive constitution. This is done with little or no concern for the larger effects
on political economy. The sense of value extended by the ethnography is not to capitalism, but to those who perforce live as the
subjects of capitalism.

In as much as choice amongst commodities has been found to
be important, it is not the range of commodities that matters, but
the exploitation of choice for extending our ability to negotiate
the ambivalences and anxieties of relationships. It is this which
can appropriate almost any amount of variation between the
stable and the innovative, the abstemious and the hedonistic, that
even the massive weight of capitalist production of commodity
symbolism can throw at us. This is not an argument for the
retention of, or extension of, choice in commodities. It is rather
an ethnographically based assessment of how it is that, given this
growth in commodities, consumers are able to assimilate them
within concerns which are generated by issues quite unrelated to
those which account for the growth in commodity choice itself.
This is why making shopping decisions much more often involves
weighing up the least bad social consequence of the decision to
be made and are only rarely the end point of some delightful
contemplation of sensual treats. This does not mean that the
experience is any the less pleasurable, but that this pleasure is
more often associated with the sense of skill involved both in
thrift and in monitoring and subtly altering relationships the
shoppers care about.[67]

In an ethnographic account I see my task as empathizing with
those whom I am trying to understand. This in no way betokens
approval of the *status quo*. The theory of shopping is based on
an ethnography which reveals quite conservative attitudes to the
family and gender. But the basic relationship of shopping to love
and sacrifice might be just as powerful if the relationships of
shoppers were primarily homosexual, communal or confluent.
In another context shopping may have little to do with love and
little in common with sacrifice. An ethnography provides a theory

of shopping, but one which may be complemented by many other theories of shopping pertinent to other times and places. Equally it produces only one perspective on women, that which emerges from the logic of this particular practice. It is a perspective that is also compatible with many other simultaneously held systems of values that construct other forms and experiences of gender.[68]

Whether the academic aim is ultimately critique or conservation, there is a preliminary requirement to struggle towards a more profound understanding of phenomena that we seem to delight in glibly dismissing. Ethnography also leaves me with a profound respect for the sheer difficulty in sustaining and moving forward the relationships within which people live,[69] the work involved in the activity of being responsible for and concerned for others and for oneself. If this involves taking seriously, as something that matters, an activity which seems to be the world's favourite object of scorn, then so much the better.

Shopping may be many things within diverse contexts. In this essay an ethnography of one North London street has provided the basis for resisting a tendency to use shopping as merely a motif in generalizing about the *Zeitgeist* or to symbolize social distinctions. The contention has been that shopping may also be a ritual practice. Its foundation is a sacrificial logic whose purpose is to constitute desiring subjects. Sacrifice was based on the rites for transforming consumption into devotion. Shopping begins with a similar rite which negates mere expenditure in obeisance to the higher purposes of thrift. It ends as the labour of constituting both the immediacy and the dynamics of specific relations of love.

Notes

1 My use of the term 'habitus', here and elsewhere in this essay, follows that of Bourdieu (1977).

2 Alison Clarke is a lecturer in the history of design at the University of Brighton, but is conducting this work as a graduate student under my supervision at the Department of Anthropology, University College London.

3 My project was also carried out as part of a larger study of two North London shopping centres. The project, called 'Consumption and Identity: a study of two North London shopping centres', was funded by the Economic and Social Research Council. It was based on a collaboration between Peter Jackson (Sheffield), Michael Rowlands (UCL) and Nigel Thrift (Bristol). The research fellow on the project was Beverley Holbrook (UCL). The overall project included questionnaires at two shopping centres and the holding of focus groups as well as my ethnography.

4 Council housing in Britain does not have the same connotation as housing projects within the United States. Until recently it represented around a third of all housing.

5 In Britain there is a general stereotyping of such housing types in relation to the class system. If anything, the previous Conservative government tended to encourage the stigmatization of households in council estates in order to persuade people to move out of state-owned property or to purchase their own accommodation. The division of council housing from owner-occupied housing is not coincident with class divisions, since there is now a large section of working-class households who are in owner-occupied accommodation.

6 The main limit to including all households on the street were the absence of some householders during the working day, and my focus, owing to family commitments, on conducting fieldwork at this time. Following the leafleting and approaching of households on Jay Road itself only fourteen of those who were able to take part during the day time completely refused to do so. This means that although the study represents some 30 percent of households in the street, it represents some 80 percent of available households. The bias this produces is clearly in favour of family-based households where the factors I dwell on in this essay would be more pronounced. This is not true of Clarke's fieldwork which is less constrained by time.

Evidence will be presented to argue for the conformity of under-represented household types, such as single-person households, to the general observations made in this essay. For example, my data are biased towards female shoppers, but there was evidence that many men in full-time work, who go grocery shopping on the weekend or in the evenings, still desire to distance themselves from any close identification with shopping as an activity and buy most goods on instruction from their female partners.

Out of the seventy-six households included, the involvement in fifty-five cases has been with females only, in fourteen cases it was with males only and in seven cases with both males and females. The family composition of those households where I feel sure of what category they fall into, is given in the table. It should be noted that the category 'single' includes households shared by several unrelated individuals. Several of those living on the council estate own their own properties but we felt the more marked differentiation remains whether one lives on a council estate or not. It will be evident that the council estates are dominated by single adults, with or without children, while the houses and maisonettes are dominated by nuclear families, although this does not necessarily imply that the adults are legally married.

	Nuclear (or extended)	Parent–Child	Two Adult	Single
Council	7	10	3	15
Non Council	19	3	1	9

In terms of ethnicity, of the seventy-six households (again I would not claim certainty in all cases) approximately nine include a person of West Indian origin, four include persons of Cypriot origin and about fourteen others a member not brought up in Britain but varying from South and East Asia to West Africa to European and South American countries. Of the remaining forty-nine households eight have a Jewish member, although in only one of these are both partners Jewish. This represents a higher proportion of English-born households than would be suggested by figures taken from the local primary school. The discrepancy is partly accounted for by eight pensioners on the council estate, who were almost all English and indeed in most cases local in origin, as against the school's bias towards families with young children.

7 For a study of the consumption of state facilities on a North London council estate see Miller 1988.

8 In an accompanying volume (Miller et al. in press) the same ethnographic material is subject to just such an analysis, with particular consideration given to the relationship between shopping and both class and ethnicity.

9 Miller 1995 provides a summary of the approaches by a wide range of disciplines to the topic of consumption and an extensive bibliography of both conventional and vanguard approaches to that topic.

10 I should repeat here my debt to Laura Rival who persuaded me to read first Richman (1982) and then Bataille (1988). I was quite reluctant, having found my previous readings of other work by Bataille to have been rather fruitless and being still more distanced from his work by its appropriation within debates on postmodernism (see Richardson 1994: 4–11).

11 Throughout this essay 'A' is the informant's answer to a question and 'Q' is the question asked. The speech is reported verbatim and I have not tried to convert it into formal grammar or 'accepted' words.

12 Examples for Britain start with Oakley (1976), and a good selection of the genre may be found collected together in Jackson and Moores (1995). Feminist research is complemented by other genres of sociological research of which Finch (1989) is a particularly important representative and whose results have largely confirmed the centrality of woman as carer and worker within the family.

13 For further details of this ambivalence as expressed in the tension between mothers and infants during shopping see Miller (in press).

14 This is notwithstanding that, according to Campbell (1986: 27), it was only in the eighteenth century that love was considered sufficient grounds for marriage in Britain. Now it is the only grounds that seems to be able to claim general legitimacy.

15 There may be a need at this point to justify (at least for a non-anthropological readership) what might be called the non-critical approach to what is after all one of the core topics to which feminist scholarship has contributed. A recent edited collection (Jackson and Moores 1995) pulls together a number of the classic articles on domestic consumption. It starts with contributions from writers such as Christine Delphy and Anne Whitehead who exposed the inequalities of economic relations and power in the household which meant that women literally worked for their families at the expense of themselves, and budgets were organized around exploitative relationships. These are followed by studies including those of Anne Murcott and Nickie Charles which explore in more detail how budgetary inequalities are then reproduced in the serving of meals which, in their deference to the husband,

seem to equate women with servants. Jackson and Moores call their collection 'critical readings', and virtually all the articles contained therein have as their objective a critique of current relationships and the feminist desire to transform these relationships in the direction of equality. To these might be added the earlier influence of Ann Oakley's (1976) pathbreaking work on the housewife and, more recently, the sensitive analysis of contradictions in women's lives by Rosalind Coward (e.g. Coward 1992). This would provide a solid guide to work in Britain and there are equivalent studies carried out by feminist researchers in other countries.

The stance taken by these articles is one I entirely support in both my politics and private life. Nevertheless this essay examines the same sets of relationships without constituting a critique. As a male author I face the obvious response that my lack of critique supports a status quo that benefits males in general and potentially me in particular. Worse still, I write as a male anthropologist and as such bear the legacy of a discipline that has been argued to have objectified the rites and practices of many peoples in such a manner as to have furthered rather than constrained the colonial project. In this case I might perhaps represent patriarchy as colonialism. This is one of the reasons I identify this essay as a work of anthropology. In practice I more often categorize my work in terms of material culture but here I am using the term 'anthropologist' to demonstrate that I am not attempting to shirk the historical responsibilities that accrue to that label.

I must also admit that I am not altogether convinced by what has become a fashionable critique (often auto-critique) of anthropology (e.g. Marcus and Fischer 1986). Modern anthropology struggled for an empathetic and holistic account of practices which humanized at least as much as it categorized peoples who were often otherwise condemned within popular and essentialized racism. Since I would rather emulate than condem Weiss it would be most consistent to adopt the same approach to a study of my own society. Furthermore it tended to be the colonial authorities (rather than the anthropologists) who took a clear stance against bride-burning, excessive dowry systems, ritual prostitution and other activities, condemned then as heathen ignorance and condemned now by feminist universalizing assertions of women's rights. Of course, each of these categories – anthropologists, colonial authorities and feminists – contain many variants who did not and do not conform to these generalizations. The primary aim of feminist research has been a critical intervention in their own society. DeVault is one of many who note the deep ideological rift between their perspective and those of many of their female informants. As such, their intervention has often been to 'raise' or 'change' consciousness. My aim is not to detract from this critique, which I share and support, just as a hundred years ago I would probably have supported the colonial desire to destroy cultural practices which I might have at that time regarded as abhorrent. (Not surprisingly, I still regard them as abhorrent.)

Anthropology in its modern form, however, rarely directed itself to critiques of this kind. Rather it has been, at least since Malinowski and Boas, an empathetic discipline that sought to understand a particular cultural practice or statement within its own terms, which meant the beliefs and values of that particular people within that particular region. The virtue of this complementary perspective is not that I believe it is somehow more objective, but because the aim is simply different: to provide understanding through a totalization of context. As such, this essay attempts to encompass both the normative ideology of housewifery and the critique by feminism as elements within a wider cosmological system that has generated both. Feminism itself is both ideological and normative in attempting to inculcate certain fundamental ideals and judgements and to make itself a general and taken-for-granted perspective.

16 Terms such as 'ideology' may be used to pinpoint the more general models and expectations we live by and for, as against any specific relationship that partially manifests them at any one time. The concept of ideology helps us to understand how there can exist both as a category and as a practice a person termed a housewife who performs devotional duties even in the absence of any particular recipient who is deemed worthy of these devotions. The term 'normative' is also used frequently in this essay in reference to this higher, more abstract level of consensual expectations that transcends the sea of diversity and contingency that is found in daily experience. The combined term 'normative ideology' returns us to a point made earlier that, in order to understand specific relationships and events, we often need to acknowledge the degree to which these manifest transcendent structures of belief and expectations, such as how parents are expected to confront and then deal with something called sibling rivalry, or the implicit values made manifest (but not usually explicit) in gifts at Christmas. These are normative not only in the sense of typical but in the sense of norms that by expressing ideology constrain and direct our actions. This is why within anthropology the simple relativism that arises from the method of ethnography where we experience every person and relationship as unique is often matched by an insistance that anthropology itself should be comparative and generalist in its use of ethnography.

17 For which topic see Pahl 1989.

18 Ibis Pond (a pseudonym) will be mentioned on several occasions in reporting the ethnography. Although the work centred on the use of Wood Green and Brent Cross, many shoppers also used Ibis Pond, which is not a separate shopping centre, but one of the many 'villages' that have developed as North London shopping districts, which tend to be dominated by relatively high-priced smaller retail outlets serving a largely middle-class clientele.

19 For the general background to these developments in British supermarkets see Bromley and Thomas (eds) 1993 and Wrigley and Lowe (eds) 1996.

20 For details of own-label branding in the British food trade see Doel 1996.

21 I am not trying to imply that such computation is beyond the ability of most shoppers. On the contrary, my qualitative observation would support the much more systematic observations by Lave, Murtaugh and de la Rocha (1984) on the arithmetics of grocery shopping. They discovered that the accuracy of shoppers when undertaking mental arithmetic in the store was 98 percent, while the very same shoppers undertaking similar problems in a formal arithmetic test achieved only 59 percent (ibid.: 82). My impression also was that even those who would not see themselves as particularly able or well educated in formal schooling were both relaxed and competent at the practical task of decision making while standing in front of supermarket shelves.

22 The degree to which what I am describing is specific to British or more local depiction is hard to determine, given the paucity of comparative ethnography. I suspect, however, that there may be a local character to this kind of thrift where set within this context of stereotypical British reticence towards expenditure. On this note it may be easier to quote the travel writer Bill Bryson since (a) he can get away with generalizations an ethnographer would blush at and (b) he is a lot funnier about them. He comments on this attribute of the British as follows:

They are the only people in the world who think of jam and currants as thrilling constituents of a pudding or cake. Offer them something genuinely tempting – a slice of gateau or a choice of chocolates from a box – and they will nearly always hesitate and begin to worry that it's unwarranted and excessive, as if any pleasure beyond a very modest threshold is vaguely unseemly.

'Oh, I shouldn't really,' they say.

'Oh, go on,' you prod encouragingly.

'Well, just a small one then,' they say and dartingly take a small one, and then get a look as if they have just done something *terribly* devilish. All this is completely alien to the American mind. To an American the whole purpose of living, the one constant confirmation of continued existence, is to cram as much sensual pleasure as possible into one's mouth more or less continuously. Gratification instant and lavish, is a birthright . . . Before long I came to regard all kinds of activities – asking for more toast at a hotel, buying wool-rich socks at Marks and Spencer, getting two pairs of trousers when I only really needed one – as something daring, very nearly illicit. My life became immensely richer. (Bryson 1996: 98–9)

23 That is, a pint of beer at the local pub.

24 For a more detailed exploration of the relationship between individuals and cultural normativity and the argument that within modernity the latter is more often based on contradiction than consistency see Miller 1994.

25 There are many gurus from Baudrillard to Bauman who may serve to characterize this academic niche.

26 Miller et al. in press, ch. 8, is a study of the differential degree of association with shopping centres based on ethnic affiliation.

27 At least up to the date of writing, 'never' in this case means never.

28 For further details see Miller et al. in press, in particular chs 3 and 4.

29 I would ruefully acknowledge that this sense of never having enough time was particularly exacerbated by the presence of an ethnographer constantly requesting time to be given for his research. But it is quite consistent with the sense of time presented in other contexts, and in my experience of North London society outside this research, and (for what it is worth) my own self-representation as a born and bred North Londoner.

30 In commenting upon this section, Colin Campbell draws attention (personal communication) to a core contrast that he observed in his study of shopping in Leeds, in the north of England. This was between shopping as work and shopping as leisure and pleasure. The latter was based around window shopping, browsing and looking for things one feels one wants rather than needs. I would confirm that at the level of discourse the latter image retains its importance (and Campbell's source material was focus groups). But my studies suggest that in day-to-day life, while many people imagine the delights of this non-provisioning shopping, outside holidays few people actually spend their time in this way. It may be that an outsider could say they don't really 'need' the actual item they spend time looking for, but shoppers tend to legitimate time as well spent in much the same way they legitimate spending as thrift. A great deal of browsing can be experienced as though it were price comparison or gaining knowledge in order to make more efficient purchases at some later date, even if no purchase actually takes place.

It may be noted that one of the 'treats' given as an example in the previous section was a group of young women going out shopping when depressed, and my findings would suggest that the actual occasions of pure shopping as pleasure are rare enough to be experienced as the treat that, as with other treats, defines the vast majority of shopping expeditions as other than leisure.

31 As it happens, I did check my newspaper (the *Guardian*) today (16 December 1996) and found on p. 3 the leading article is called 'Don't Go Mad, Go Shopping' and is based on recent academic research on 'shopaholics' with photos of Ivana Trump, Elton John and the Duchess of York who represent precisely the image of the 'true shopper' being described here. On the same day the front page of the *Guardian*'s 'G2' section consists of a picture of a supermarket for religions called 'Religiomart' and the story (pp. 2–3) bemoans the rise of 'pick'n'mix' religion. I remain confident that on whatever day you happen to be reading this, your own newspaper is likely to provide its own additional material to reinforce this point.

32 An honourable exception is an article entitled 'The Science of Shopping' (*New Yorker* 4 Nov. 1996: 66–75). This provides a well-researched summary of the latest techniques by which commerce studies shopping, such as observing videos and calculating the precise examination of products, and developing 'types' of shoppers. Unusually, however, the article is clear about

how little such information can be used to manipulate shoppers into making purchases they would not otherwise have made. It admits to 'a new humility in shopping theory'. This suggests that the situation is not so different in the United States from that in Trinidad, where I found marketing and advertising to be similarly limited in their effects (Miller 1997; see also Schudson 1984).

33 Not only in our time. Berry (1994) has recently documented the long history of a concern with luxury. Of particular interest is the highly gendered discourse on male asceticism and effeminate profligacy that dominated both Greek and Roman concerns over materialism (ibid.: 59, 77).

34 This discussion can be directed equally well at those who follow a religious life and believe in a transcendent other, with which sacrifice creates a relationship, as it fits a secular understanding in which sacrifice, by purporting to be a relationship, is actually constituting its 'taken-for-granted' object of devotion.

35 Such slaughters may still occur, but as far as can be ascertained from biblical sources, none of the animals had BSE.

36 For an earlier emphasis upon this aspect of sacrifice see Robertson Smith (1894).

37 This example is not strictly comparable since it deals with consecration rather than sacrifice *per se*, but there seems little reason to doubt that the symbolic logic revealed in the consideration of *prasad* is directly analogous with that being extracted by modern scholars from ancient Greek sacrifice. The practices involving *prasad* and *jutha* also vary by region and group. The description offered here is based on ethnographic observation within a particular region by Parry (1979).

38 A ritual feast held by Amerindians of the northwest coast of America once assumed to be based on the competitive destruction of valuables.

39 The more rigid versions of Marxism would provide other examples of this phenomenon.

Since this clearly implies a personal stance from which Bataille would stand condemned, I should perhaps be explicit about what these days is called 'where I am coming from'. My own academic conceptualization of humanity is derived mainly from the reworking of Hegel and Judaism by Rose (1992, 1993, 1996). I would wish to follow her conclusion that the highest achievement of humanity is law as an objectification of the inherent contradictions of ethics, which is where, if anywhere, we attempt something which might be called a relationship to the divine.

40 The Kula ring consists of an elaborate form of circulation of armshells and necklaces between the populations of a group of islands off the coast of Papua New Guinea. The Kula has been one of the best known case studies in anthropological analysis since it was first reported in considerable detail by Malinowski in his *Argonauts of the Western Pacific* (1922).

41 Objectification is the term I have used to appropriate a vulgar version of the dialectical theory found in Hegel's *Phenomenology* (1977). This holds that

culture can only result from the self-alienation of human creativity and its consequent sublation as the expansion of the potentiality of humanity. I have previously argued (Miller 1987) that this account of the Kula may be taken as exemplary of such a 'Hegelian' approach to a theory of culture. The same may be said of sacrifice which is here shown to follow the same logic whereby humanity alienates an aspect of itself identified with the sacrificial victim and gives this up to a transcendent realm of the divine. This comes back to humanity in the form of religious belief and culture. It is likely that Hegel and later religious commentators would see this as merely a stage towards more abstract forms by which one gains consciousness of the divine (Hegel 1977: 453–78).

42 A number of the papers in de Grazia (1996) contribute to an understanding of the historical process by which consumption came to be gendered to the degree that is common today.

43 For the details of a theory of objectification as a dialectic of subjects and objects see Miller (1987).

44 Mainstream studies that classify shoppers for commercial purposes are found in profusion in journals such as *Advances in Consumer Research* and the *Journal of Retail Studies*, and in contributions from psychologists (see Lunt and Livingstone 1992 ch. 5). Ignoring the consumer in favour of the study of business technologies of manipulation is found in historical and Marxist studies such as Haug 1986 and Williams 1982. More promising are some recent studies by retail geographers that tend to be well informed and balanced in their critical analysis, though the emphasis is on retail rather than shopper development (e.g. Bromley and Thomas 1993, Wrigley and Lowe 1996).

45 This accusation may be levelled at actual studies of shopping ranging from the highly positivist study of consumer behaviour in formal consumer studies to a tendency to focus upon major shopping malls and topics such as fantasy and postmodernism in sociological and geographical studies of shopping (e.g. Chaney 1990, Goss 1993, Shields 1992). The latter tendency is exacerbated by the still more influential works of grand social theory which tends to treat consumption as a more general trope for assertions about the so-called postmodern world (e.g. Baudrillard 1983 and Bauman 1990, 1991).

46 As was the case with the discussion of sacrifice, the intention is not to attempt to define a universal form of love or even to consider whether love is indeed universal. It is rather to try to understand the cosmological significance of the love observed in North London shopping as against its cultural contextualization elsewhere. There certainly exists anthropological speculation on the universality of love and, in particular, romantic passion. A recent work edited by Jankowiak (1995) is explicitly directed at this question. Most of the papers in that volume argue for the universal presence of romantic passion, as against the assumption that this is a particular historical outcome of the Romantic movement. For example, Harris (1995) argues

that despite the stress on sexuality *per se* in the anthropological literature on Polynesian societies, there is other evidence that romantic love is clearly present and significant. On the other hand, Birth and Freilich (1995) argue that in Trinidad (and by implication much of the rest of the Caribbean) sexuality was for quite some time relatively unfounded in ideas of romantic love, which have tended to emerge only with the influence of television and other media where romantic love is a core genre. My own research in Trinidad would tend to confirm this (Miller 1994). The stance taken here, therefore, depends upon a historical and relativistic perspective on love, in which, as with sacrifice, we might create generalizations but do not assume universals.

47 Or even in quite different settings such as the study by Trawick (1990) of love in a South Indian Tamil context.

48 Potentially, of course, either partner, but despite the avowed feminism, it was almost invariably the mother.

49 Using evidence from another area of consumption, the genres of advertising Goffman (1979), produced a fascinating argument which goes in the opposite direction to derive the structure of gender asymmetry in partnerships from the normative ideals of parental care and power.

50 The same point may be noted in justification of this essay as empathetic of the *status quo* rather than constituting a critique. I have no desire to preserve this *status quo*, but if the rhetoric of condemnation has been largely unsuccessful in creating the conditions for change, then it may be that what is required first is a fuller and more empathetic appreciation of the factors that contribute to this conservatism.

51 Weiner's critique is partly aimed at those who used the exchange of women between social groups as their core example. In her study the focus is turned instead to the role of women in many societies as the devotees that maintain the power of the inalienable by standing for that which cannot be reduced to exchange. A core example is woman as sibling rather than woman as wife, though she acknowledges the problematic status of love as passionate devotion when applied within the sibling relation (ibid.: 76–7). The implication is that as both devotees and as objects of devotion, the love that women are responsible for is at the core of what constitutes the inalienable possession.

The most obvious contrast to Weiner's emphasis in the study of women must be that of Strathern, and both have been explicit in contrasting their analyses of women with each other (e.g. Weiner ibid.: 14–15, Strathern 1981). Irrespective of whether either author considers herself to be a feminist, the differences in their approach seem clearly to expound upon what was at that time a major conflict within feminist ideology. From this perspective, Strathern appears as a major anthropological exponent of what might be termed 'deconstructive feminism'. Her concern was to critique the very concept of gender. Deconstructive feminism is itself a logical outcome of modernity as an attack on all pre-given systems of difference and on the ideologies from which these supposed differences were supported. Seen from the perspective of Weiner, this is understood as turning the study of exchange established by Mauss and Lévi-Strauss into a still more general model of sheer equivalence, that demolishes in turn, society, the individual or any other essentialized category in the quest for basic elements which can be subjected to exchange and equivalence. In the face of such an onslaught, given categories such as female and male fall away. This thereby becomes an exemplary instance of the process which (following upon the influence of Derrida) tends to be termed 'deconstruction'.

Within anthropology, Strathern's (1988) book *The Gender of the Gift* allowed for the full development of this deconstruction of gender in the name of equivalence. A key motif in her book is its refusal of the particular Western grounding of value in labour in order to concentrate on value created in exchange, which is central to Melanesian conceptions of value. Although Strathern is vitally concerned with the issue of commensurability, it is not the case that she is simply accepting a world of equivalence. She appears equally concerned with the search for and nature of incommensurability in Western as much as in Melanesian society. The issue of incommensurability is understood as of increasing significance in the context of what seem ever-growing networks of equivalence.

Weiner, by contrast, when viewed from the perspective of Strathern becomes clearly emblematic of another equally important strand within the feminist critique. Instead of trying to deconstruct gender itself, the quest here is to excavate the hidden ramifications of what is being objectified in the feminine, as culturally constituted. Weiner's starting-point as an anthropologist was rather that women – their activities and their significance – had been ignored. Within feminist contexts this is often taken as implying that there are key qualities which women retain by virtue of the way culture has objectified gender, and which if moved from the background to the foreground of political and ethical debate might improve and enhance our lives. Returned to the case of inalienable objects, Weiner's concern is to foreground the importance of women in many societies, in retaining and maintaining the inalienable and the transcendent, rather than seeing women merely as agents of sexuality and expenditure.

There is a clear link between the emphasis on exchange as foundation for the production of value in Melanesia and the political insistence upon equivalence in the feminist critique of the domestic household in the West. This is evident in works such as DeVault's (1991) *Feeding the Family*. Almost despite herself, DeVault's text emphasizes how at the heart of capitalism is a domestic world in which there is a constant refusal to see relationships in terms of effort and contribution. Yet the critique she espouses is based precisely upon the uncovering of equivalence, or more importantly lack of equivalence, in domestic labour.

DeVault's attempt to excavate the hidden labour of domestic work in the name of a principle of fairness of exchange in gender relations was typical of a range of feminist studies of domestic labour. In the 1990s such work has begun to be overtaken by a literature which focuses more on love and sexuality and on the ambivalent nature of both their practice and of the feminist critique itself (for a summary of the internal debate within feminism on the issue of sexuality see Segal 1994). Taken in the context of the dynamics of feminist concerns, the theory of shopping oulined here has the effect of connecting a primary topic of recent debate back to the context of the study of household labour, which as a genre dominated earlier feminist research.

52 *Toanga* and *tjurunga* are both forms of sacred valuables and inalienable possessions.

53 Interestingly, this seems to have as much to do with the medieval European house as it does with the Kwakiutl of the northwest coast of America.

54 For which see Netting, Wilk and Arnould 1984.

55 Several papers in de Grazia (1996) provide historical documentation for the development of the modern house as a unit of consumption. This becomes part of the more general development of the domestic sphere documented by Davidoff and Hall (1987: 380–8).

56 For details of the various disciplinary approaches to this question see Miller 1995.

57 See for example Schudson (1984), and for a case study Miller (1997: ch. 4). For a counter-argument see Fine and Leopold 1993.

58 Sometimes shopping is for an object that will symbolize relationships as categories, as when we mark the relationship to a cousin or friend at a specific event such as Christmas or a wedding through giving a gift. Here the gift is the sign of that relationship and the primary concern is that it should be appropriate to it.

59 This assumes a constellation of such brands. There may not be so much resting on any particular brand, which is why, when faced with the competing possibility of thrift, supermarket own-label goods may over time replace such brands. On the other hand, the supermarkets may then insinuate themselves into a similar niche of nostalgia, so that the dinner-party conversation turns to how 'I shop at Sainsbury just like my mother did' where the shop itself becomes the brand. One of the main uses being made of this tradition (at least in Britain) can be found in the rise of local museums of social history, where older versions of such brands often play a major role in the dioramas which portray life in the 1930s or the 1960s etc.

60 This quality may become linked with whatever is still retained of much older associations between a sense of the sacred and commodities or more particularly money itself (see Belk and Wallendorf 1990, Carrier 1995b: 168–89).

61 It should be noted that the subjects in this passage are not individuals *per se*, but persons constantly being (re)defined by their social relationships.

62 For further details of this argument see Miller 1987.

63 Thanks are due to Webb Keane for helping to clarify this point.

64 The ethnography suggested that, although men may be increasingly engaged in shopping, they retain their ability to distance themselves from shopping. On the other hand, historical surveys suggest that, if anything, women are becoming responsible for more rather than fewer areas of shopping choice. 'It would be difficult to ignore women's increasing importance as purchasers of those consumer goods that had been regarded traditionally as 'masculine' and/or gender free. Once again the 1960s seemed to constitute something of a turning point . . . Thus women shoppers ended the period more visible, and no doubt more powerful, than they had ever been before' (Benson 1994: 73–4).

65 It is worth noting that the degree of emphasis upon the family in this essay by no means implies that people enjoy shopping with their family. In another account we have argued that most shoppers show a clear dislike of shopping together with other family members, yet nevertheless collude with the commercial owners of shopping centres in making the centres strive to be seen as ideal habitats for family shopping. One of the reasons for this contradiction that emerges from the present study is that the desired family member is one who can be imagined as the deserving recipient of the labour of shopping. This is a projection that may be difficult to sustain in the face of the bored and irritable companion who is having to accompany the shopper (for details of this argument see Miller et al. in press, ch. 5).

Nevertheless this claim is based on the finding that most people on the street are mainly concerned with a few relationships which dominate their lives. This claim seems to be entirely consistent with the weight of sociological research on the family and friendship in modern Britain. In summarizing research on these topics, Allan (1996) refutes the assertion that today's individuals are more isolated than they used to be in earlier generations (ibid.: 18), and notes that 'the home and the domestic relationships entailed in it are highly significant for the majority of people throughout most life-course phases' (ibid.: 129).

66 Modern theology would, however, suggest parallel developments in its conceptualization of the relationship to God from a more fixed to a more fluid form.

67 This point is even more evident when one considers cooking as domestic labour. In general this is only ever seen as a pleasurable activity when it is clearly being undertaken on behalf of others. There is no reason to assume that shopping or cooking for the self is liable to be more pleasurable than labour on behalf of others, given the overwhelming concern for relationships. The ethnography demonstrated the existence of a longer-term sense of pleasure from shopping, as long as it has been recognized for its contribution to the household, held alongside the more immediate pleasure of shopping as the treat, the highly individualistic and unconstrained browsing for oneself.

68 On the plurality of discourses on gender see Moore 1994.

69 One result of this has been the emphasis upon care and sensitivity in household relations. This may appear to have led to a neglect of issues of power, but while I acknowledge that power is an element of all such relations, the ethnographic experience suggested that it is the devotional aspects of love that have been underrepresented in the critical literature.

Bibliography

Alexiou, M. 1990 'Reappropriating Greek sacrifice', *Journal of Modern Greek Studies* 8: 97–123.

Allan, G. 1996 *Kinship and Friendship in Modern Britain*. Oxford: Oxford University Press.

Auslander, L. 1996 'The gendering of consumer practices in nineteenth-century France'. In de Grazia 1996.

Bataille, G. 1987 *Eroticism*. London: Marion Boyars.

Bataille, G. 1988 *The Accursed Share*. New York: Zone Books.

Bataille, G. 1990 'Hegel, death and sacrifice', *Yale French Studies* 78: 9–28.

Baudrillard, J. 1981 *For a Critique of the Political Economy of the Sign*. St. Louis: Telos Press.

Baudrillard, J. 1983 *Simulations*. New York: Semiotext(e).

Bauman, Z. 1990 *Thinking Sociologically*. Oxford: Blackwell.

Bauman, Z. 1991 *Modernity and Ambivalence*. Cambridge: Polity.

Beck, U. and Beck-Gernsheim, E. 1995 *The Normal Chaos of Love*. Cambridge: Polity.

Beidelman, T. 1974 *W. Robertson Smith and the Sociological Study of Religion*. Chicago: University of Chicago Press.

Belk, R. and Coon, G. 1993 'Gift-giving as agapic love: an alternative to the exchange paradigm based on dating experiences', *Journal of Consumer Research* 20: 393–417.

Belk, R. and Wallendorf, M. 1990 'The sacred meanings of money', *Journal of Economic Psychology* 11: 35–67.

Benson, J. 1994 *The Rise of Consumer Society in Britain* 1880–1980. Harlow: Longman.

Berry, C. 1994 *The Idea of Luxury*. Cambridge: Cambridge University Press.

Birth, K. and Freilich, M. 1995 'Putting romance into systems of sexuality: changing smart rules in a Trinidadian village'. In Jankowiak 1995.

Bloch, M. 1992 *Prey into Hunter*. Cambridge: Cambridge University Press.

Bourdieu, P. 1977 *Outline of a Theory of Practice*. Cambridge: Cambridge University Press.

Bourdieu, P. 1984 *Distinction: A Social Critique of the Judgement of Taste*. London: Routledge and Kegan Paul.

Bourdieu, P. 1996 *The Rules of Art*. Cambridge: Polity.

Bromley, D. and Thomas, C. (eds) 1993 *Retail Change: contemporary issues*. London: UCL Press.

Bryson, B. 1996 *Notes From a Small Island*. London: Black Swan.

Burke, T. 1996 *Lifebuoy Men, Lux Women*. Durham, NC: Duke University Press.

Burkert, W. 1983 *Homo Necans*. Berkeley: University of California Press.

Campbell, C. 1986 *The Romantic Ethic and the Spirit of Modern Consumerism*. Oxford: Blackwell.

Campbell, C. forthcoming 'Shopping pleasure and the context of desire'. In van Beek, G. and Govers, C. (eds) *The Global and the Local: Consumption and European Identity*. Amsterdam: Spinhuis Press.

Carrier, J. (ed.) 1995a *Occidentalism*. Oxford: Oxford University Press.

Carrier, J. 1995b *Gifts and Commodities: Exchange and Western Capitalism since 1700*. London: Routledge.

Carsten, J. and Hugh-Jones, S. 1995 *About the House*. Cambridge: Cambridge University Press.

Chaney, D. 1990 'Dystopia in Gateshead: the metrocentre as a cultural form', *Theory, Culture and Society* 7: 4.

Charles, N. and Kerr, M. 1988 *Women, Food and Families*. Manchester: Manchester University Press.

Clarke, A. 1997 'Window shopping at home: classifieds, catalogues and new consumer skills'. In Miller 1993.

Clarke, A. forthcoming *Tupperware: design and domesticity*. Washington: Smithsonian Institute Press.

Coward, R. 1992 *Our Treacherous Hearts: Why Women Let Men Get Their Way*. London: Faber and Faber.

Daunton, M. 1983 *House and Home in the Victorian City: working-class housing 1850–1914*. London: Edward Arnold.

Davidoff, L. and Hall, C. 1987 *Family Fortunes*. London: Hutchinson.

de Grazia, V. (ed.) 1996 *The Sex of Things*. Berkeley: University of California Press.

de Heusch, L. 1985 *Sacrifice in Africa*. Manchester: Manchester University Press.

Detienne, M. 1989 'Culinary practices and the spirit of sacrifice'. In Detienne and Vernant 1989.

Detienne, M. and Vernant, J.-P. (eds) 1989 *The Cuisine of Sacrifice among the Greeks*. Chicago: University of Chicago Press.

DeVault, M. 1991 *Feeding the Family*. Chicago: University of Chicago Press.

Doel, C. 1996 'Market development and organizational change: the case of the food industry'. In Wrigley and Lowe 1996.

Douglas, M. and Isherwood, B. 1979 *The World of Goods*. London: Allen Lane.

Dumont, L. 1970 *Homo Hierarchichus*. London: Weidenfeld and Nicolson.

Featherstone, M. 1991 *Consumer Culture and Postmodernism*. London: Sage.

Finch, J. 1989 *Family Obligations and Social Change*. Cambridge: Polity.

Fine, B. and Leopold, E. 1993 *The World of Consumption*. London: Routledge.

Frykman, J. and Lofgren, O. 1987 *Culture Builders*. New Brunswick: Rutgers University Press.

Gay, P. 1992 'The manliness of Christ'. In R. Davis and R. Helmstadter (eds) *Religion and Irreligion in Victorian Society*. London: Routledge.

Gell, A. 1992 'Technology and magic', *Anthropology Today*: 4.

Giddens, A. 1992 *The Transformation of Intimacy*. Cambridge: Polity.

Girard, R. 1977 *Violence and the Sacred*. Baltimore: John Hopkins Press.

Gladwell, M. 1996 'The science of shopping', *New Yorker* 4 Nov.: 66–75.

Goffman, E. 1975 *Frame Analysis*. Harmondsworth: Penguin.

Goffman, E. 1979 *Gender Advertisements*. London: Macmillan.

Goss, J. 1993 'The "magic of the mall": an analysis of form, function, and meaning in the contemporary retail built environment', *Annals, Association of American Geographers* 83: 18–47.

Gudeman, S. and Rivera, A. 1990 *Conversations in Colombia*. Cambridge: Cambridge University Press.

Hamerton-Kelly, R. 1987 (ed.) *Violent Origins*. Stanford: Stanford University Press.

Harris, H. 1995 'Rethinking heterosexual relationships in Polynesia'. In Jankowiak 1995.

Haug, W. 1986 *Critique of Commodity Aesthetics*. Cambridge: Polity.

Hegel, G. 1977 [1807] *Phenomenology of Spirit*. Oxford: Oxford University Press.

Hubert, H. and Mauss, M. 1964 *Sacrifice: its nature and functions*. Chicago: University of Chicago Press.

Hugh-Jones, S. 1992 'Yesterday's luxuries, tomorrow's necessities: business and barter in northwest Amazonia'. In Humphrey, C. and Hugh-Jones, S. (eds) *Barter, Exchange and Value*. Cambridge: Cambridge University Press.

Jackson, S. and Moores, S. (eds) 1995 *The Politics of Domestic Consumption: critical readings*. London: Prentice Hall.

Jankowiak, W. (ed.) 1995 *Romantic Passion*. New York: Columbia University Press.

Kopytoff, I. 1986 'The cultural biography of things: commoditization as process'. In Appadurai, A. (ed.) *The Social Life of Things*. Cambridge: Cambridge University Press.

Lave, J., Murtaugh, M. and de la Rocha, A. 1984 'The dialectic of arithmetic in grocery shopping'. In Rogoff, B. and Lave, J. (eds) *Everyday Cognition: Its Development in Social Context*. Cambridge, Mass.: Harvard University Press.

Levine, B. 1989 *Leviticus: the JPS Torah commentary*. Philadelphia: Jewish Publication Society.

Lindholm, C. 1995 'Love as an experience of transcendence'. In Jankowiak, 1995.

Locke, J. 1970 *Two Treatises on Government*, ed. P. Laslett. Cambridge: Cambridge University Press.

Lunt, P. and Livingstone, S. 1992 *Mass Consumption and Personal Identity*. Buckingham: Open University Press.

Macfarlane, A. 1987 *The Culture of Capitalism*. Oxford: Blackwell.

Malinowski, B. 1922 *Argonauts of the Western Pacific*. London: Routledge and Kegan Paul.

Malinowski, B. 1935 *Coral Gardens and their Magic*. New York: American Book Company.

Marcus, G. and Fischer, M. 1986 *Anthropology as Cultural Critique*. Chicago: University of Chicago Press.

Marriot, M. 1968 'Caste ranking and food transactions: a matrix analysis'. In Singer, M. and Cohen, B. (eds) *Structure and Change in Indian Society*. Chicago: Aldine Publishing Company.

Marx, K. 1975 *Early Writings*. Harmondsworth: Penguin.

Mauss, M. 1966 *The Gift*. London: Cohen and West.

Milgrom, J. 1983 *Studies in Cultic Theology and Terminology*. Leiden: E. J. Brill.

Milgrom J. 1989 *Numbers: the JPS Torah commentary*. Philadelphia: Jewish Publication Society.

Milgrom, J. 1991 Leviticus 1–16. New York: Doubleday.

Miller, D. 1987 *Material Culture and Mass Consumption*. Oxford: Blackwell.

Miller, D. 1988 'Appropriating the state on the council estate'. *Man* 23: 353–72.

Miller, D. (ed.) 1993 *Unwrapping Christmas*. Oxford: Oxford University Press.

Miller, D. 1994 *Modernity: An Ethnographic Approach*. Oxford: Berg.

Miller, D. 1995 'Consumption as the vanguard of history'. In Miller, D. (ed.) *Acknowledging Consumption*. London: Routledge.

Miller, D. 1997 *Capitalism: An Ethnographic Approach*. Oxford: Berg.

Miller, D. forthcoming 'How infants grow mothers in North London', *Theory, Culture and Society*.

Miller, D., Jackson, P., Holbrook, B., Thrift, N. and Rowlands, M. in press *Shopping, Place and Identity*. London: Routledge.

Moore, H. 1994 *A Passion for Difference: essays on anthropology and gender*. Cambridge: Polity.

Munn, N. 1986 *The Fame of Gawa*. Cambridge: Cambridge University Press.

Murcott, A. 1983. '"It's a pleasure to cook for him": food, mealtimes and gender in some south Wales households'. In Garmarnikow, E., Morgan, D., Purvis, J., and Tatlorson, D. (eds) *The Public and the Private*. London: Heinemann.

Netting, R., Wilk, R. and Arnould, E. (eds) 1984 *Households: comparative and historical studies of the domestic group*. Berkeley: University of California Press.

Oakley, A. 1976 *Housewife*. Harmondsworth: Penguin.

Pahl, J. 1984 *Divisions of Labour*. Oxford: Blackwell.

Pahl, J. 1989 *Money and Marriage*. London: Macmillan.

Pahl, J. and Wallace, C. 1988 'Neither angels in marble nor rebels in red: privatization and working-class consciousness'. In Rose, D. (ed.) *Social Stratification and Economic Change*. London: Hutchinson.

Parker, R. 1996 *Torn in Two: the experience of maternal ambivalence*. London: Virago.

Parry, J. 1979 *Caste and Kinship in Kangra*. London: Routledge and Kegan Paul.

Pendergrast, M. 1993 *For God, Country and Coca-Cola*. London: Weidenfeld and Nicolson.

Reynolds, J. 1993 'The proliferation of the planned retail centre'. In Bromley and Thomas, 1993.

Richardson, M. 1994 *Georges Bataille*. London: Routledge.

Richman, M. 1982 *Beyond the Gift: Reading George Bataille*. Baltimore: Johns Hopkins.

Robertson Smith, W. 1894 *Lectures on the Religion of the Semites* (2nd edn). London: A. and C. Black.

Rosaldo, R. 1987 'Anthropological Commentary'. In Hamerton-Kelly 1987.

Rose, G. 1992 *The Broken Middle*. Oxford: Blackwell.

Rose, G. 1993 *Judaism and Modernity*. Oxford: Blackwell.

Rose, G. 1996 *Mourning Becomes the Law*. Cambridge: Cambridge University Press.

Rowlands, M. forthcoming 'Memory, sacrifice and the nation'. *New Formations*.

Ryan, A. 1982 *Property and Social Theory*. Oxford: Blackwell.

Sahlins, M. 1972 'The original affluent society'. In Sahlins, M. *Stone Age Economics*. London: Tavistock.

Sahlins, M. 1976 *Culture and Practical Reason*. Chicago: University of Chicago Press.

Schama, S. 1993 'Perishable commodities: Dutch still-life painting and the empire of things'. In Brewer, J. and Porter, R. (eds) *Consumption and the World of Things*. London: Routledge.

Schneider, D. 1968 *American Kinship: a cultural account*. Englewood Cliffs, NJ: Prentice Hall.

Schudson, M. 1984 *Advertising: the uneasy persuasion*. New York: Basic Books.

Segal, L. 1994 *Straight Sex: the politics of pleasure*. London: Virago.

Sennett, R. 1976 *The Fall of Public Man*. Cambridge: Cambridge University Press.

Sheilds, R. 1989 'Social spatialization and the built environment: West Edmonton Mall', *Environment and Planning D: Society and Space* 7: 147–64.

Shields, R. 1992 *Lifestyle Shopping: the subject of consumption*. London: Routledge.

Shorter, E. 1975 *The Making of the Modern Family*. New York: Basic Books.

Simmel, G. 1978 *The Philosophy of Money*. London: Routledge.

Slater, D. 1997 *Consumer Culture and Modernity*. Cambridge: Polity.

Smith A. 1976 [1776] *An Inquiry into the Nature and Causes of the Wealth of Nations*. Chicago: Chicago University Press.

Steedman, C. 1995 *Strange Dislocations*. Cambridge, Mass.: Harvard University Press.

Stone, L. 1977 *The Family, Sex and Marriage in England 1500–1800*. London: Weidenfeld and Nicolson.

Strathern, M. 1981 'Culture in a netbag. The manufacture of a subdiscipline in anthropology'. *Man* 16: 665–88.

Strathern, M. 1988 *The Gender of the Gift*. Berkeley: University of California Press.

Trawick, M. 1990 *Notes on Love in a Tamil Family*. Berkeley: University of California Press.

Valeri, V. 1985 *Kingship and Sacrifice*. Chicago: University of Chicago Press.

Vickery, A. 1993 'Women and the world of goods: a Lancashire consumer and her possessions 1751–81. In Brewer, J. and Porter, R. (eds) *Consumption and the World of Things*. London: Routledge.

Warde, A. 1997 *Consumption, Food and Taste*. London: Sage.

Warner, M. 1976 *Alone of All Her Sex*. London: Weidenfeld and Nicolson.

Weiner, A. 1992 *Inalienable Possessions*. Berkeley: University of California Press.

Weiss, B. 1996 *The Making and the Unmaking of the Haya Lived World*. Durham, NC: Duke University Press.

Williams, R. H. 1982 *Dream Worlds: mass consumption in late nineteenth-century France*. Berkeley and Los Angeles: University of California Press.

Wrigley, N. and Lowe, M. (eds) 1996 *Retailing, Consumption and Capital*. London: Longman.

Index

Abraham, 114
advertising, 52
Akedah, 114–15
Allan, G., 168
ancestors, 33
anthropology, 36, 67, 159–60
Argos, 54
Auslander, L., 139

Balzac, H. de., 140
Bataille, G., 6, 84–9, 92–3, 95, 98,
    104, 129, 158, 163
    The Accursed Share, 84, 86
    on consumption, 85, 93
    on eroticism, 86, 97
Beck, U. and Beck-Gernsheim, E.,
    119, 120, 122, 123
Belk, R. and Coon, C., 123
Benson, J., 168
Berry, C., 163
Bloch, M., 74, 81, 89
Bourdieu, P., 140
brands, 26, 52, 142, 167

and change, 142
own label, 51–2
and stability, 142
Britishness, 26, 56, 161
Bryson, B., 161
Burke, T., 139
busy, 69–70

Campbell, C., 69, 117, 158, 162
capitalism, 84, 88, 97, 133, 139,
    142, 153–4
Carsten, J. and Hugh-Jones, S.,
    133–4
cheapjacks, 57, 61
Christianity, 74, 115, 118
Christmas, 33, 54
Clarke, A., viii–ix, 9–10, 55–6,
    156
class, 57, 140
Colombia, 132
colonialism, 159
commodification, 139
cooking, 16, 21, 36–7, 107

consumption, 91, 97, 131–2, 136,
  138, 147, 164
  and choice, 138, 154
  by infants, 124–5
council housing, 10, 15, 23, 32,
  156, 157
Coward, R., 159
culture, 67

Davidoff, L. and Hall, C., 117–18
Day of Atonement, 77
death, 87
de Heusch, L., 79
deity, 75, 78, 99, 114, 148–9
depression, 46, 62–3
desire, 21, 71, 139, 148–9
destruction, 75–6
Detienne, M., 80, 81, 98
  and Vernant, J.-P., 80, 105
DeVault, M., 37–8, 107, 109–10,
  159, 166–7
devotion, 75, 108
  to infants, 126
diet, 46, 143
Disney, 142–3
domesticity, 136
Douglas, M. and Isherwood, B., 140

economics, 136
elderly, 32–3, 102, 121
equality, 38
ethnicity, 157
ethnography, 9, 67, 68, 69, 155, 157
exchange, 129, 166
expenditure, 76, 82, 83, 90–5, 138
  American, 161
extravagance, 45–6, 60

family meals, 44, 107
fashion, 142
feminist research, 20, 22, 38, 44,
  95, 106, 109, 126–7, 149–50,
  158, 159
  deconstructive, 165–6

fetishism, 128, 152
Finch, J., 138, 158
Fine, B. and Leopold, E., 143
focus groups, 69
football stripes, 26
Frykman, J. and Lofgren, O., 135

gender, 22, 23, 30, 39, 44, 95–6,
  118, 127, 149, 166
Giddens, A., 119, 122, 152
gift, 33, 102, 129, 131, 151, 167
Girard, R., 88–9, 97–8
Goffman, E., 165
Green movement, 97
Guardian, 162
Gudeman, S. and Rivera, A., 132–4

habitus, 8, 149
Haya, 36–7, 38
hedonism, 63, 64–5, 68, 71, 117
Hegel, G., 87, 163–4
Heinz tomato soup, 142
'house', the, 102, 132–4
households, 33, 106, 134, 135, 157
  single-person, 32–5, 48, 62,
  120–2, 157
housewives, 15, 18, 20–1, 22, 37,
  43, 96, 106, 143
Hubert, H. and Mauss, M., 6,
  75–6, 78, 94, 105
Hugh-Jones, S., 71
husbands, 44–5, 56, 144

Ibsen, H., 27
identity, 139, 141
ideology, 66, 160
IKEA, 28, 29
inalienability, 131, 146–7
inalienable possessions, 8, 129–30,
  152
individualism, 12, 32, 34, 120–2
  English, 116
individuality, 24, 42, 48
infants, 124–7, 152

James, H., 141
Jay road, 10, 11, 67, 157
John Lewis, 57
journalism, 70–1, 97
Judaism, 114–15, 163
jutha, 81, 163

Keynes, J., 133
Kula ring, 91, 163

Lévi-Strauss, C., 133, 134
Lindholm, C., 122–3
Locke, J., 130–1
loneliness, 34
love, 18–19, 20, 21, 22–3, 26–7,
     35–6, 127, 149, 150, 152–3,
     164
   'agapic', 123
   ambivalence in, 19, 31, 122, 149,
     150
   for children, 110, 124–7
   'confluent', 119, 152
   'eros', 123
   experimental, 119
   as female, 108, 149, 165
   history of, 116–19
   looking for, 121
   modern, 119–23
   and objects, 129–30
   and power, 150, 153
   and religion, 118
   Romantic, 116–17, 165
luxury, 162

Macfarlane, A., 116, 118, 132
malls, 68, 69
market, 54
Marks & Spencer, 43–4, 109
Marx, K., 131, 152, 154
material culture, 128, 138–48
materialism, 31, 34, 63, 68, 71, 125
Mauss, M., 86, 128–9, 131
Melanesia, 165–6
methodology, 10–11
middle class, 27, 43, 57, 125

Milgrom, J., 82
modernity, 147
money, 94
mothers, 124–7, 152
Munn, N., 91

National Childbirth Trust, 125
national lottery, 25
New Yorker, 162–3
normative, 160
North London, 2, 12, 113–14, 122,
     160

Oakley, A., 159
objectification, 92, 141, 151, 163–4

Pacific, 129–30
Pahl, R., 136
Parker, R., 19
Parry, J., 81, 163
patriarchy, 117–18, 126, 149
postmodernism, 96, 164
potlach, 86, 129
poverty, 31–2
power, 150, 169
prasad, 80–1, 163
price comparison, 49–51, 53, 59,
     60, 161, 162
price knowledge, 51
private housing, 15
property, 131

relativism, 11
retailing, 51–2, 54, 160, 164
reward, 40–8
Richardson, M., 87
Richman, M., 86
Rival, L., ix, 158
Romantic movement, 116
Rose, G., 163
Rowlands, M., 130

sacrifice
   African, 79, 80
   aims of, 76–7, 78, 99

analogy with shopping, 111–13
Aztec, 85–6
Christian, 74, 115
and communal meal, 80, 81, 82, 105–6
as consumption, 82, 83, 84–5, 90–4
as devotional ritual, 78
discourse of, 89–93
duality in, 99–100
first-fruit, 91
Greek, 77, 79–80, 98, 105
in Hawaii, 99
Hindu, 80–1, 99
Judaic, 77, 80, 82, 98, 115
meaning of word, 12–13, 74
mundane, 98
range of, 76–7
sacralization of, 76, 94
smoke from, 99
and social categories, 139–40
social order, 106
structure, 75–6, 94
theories of, 74–90
and violence, 80, 86, 88–9, 92–4, 98
Safeway, 52
sales, 54–5
Schneider, D., 118
self, 46–7
semiotics, 140
Sennett, R., 139, 140
sexuality, 63, 167
shopaholics, 162
shopping
    analogy with sacrifice, 111–13
    arithmetics of, 161
    for children, 17, 124, 144–5
    with children, 42–3, 145
    for clothing, 59, 109
    contradictions of, 143–6
    cosmology of, 94
    as courtship, 29–30
    discourse of, 65–72, 95–6, 100, 162

eating while, 42–3
    educative, 18, 38
    as female, 39
    for family, 37, 107–8, 168
    for food, 17, 21, 24, 26, 30, 41, 43, 50, 143
    for furniture, 27–8
    and leisure/pleasure, 68–9, 162, 168
    men, 16, 25, 39, 44–5, 104, 109, 122, 144, 168
    mundane, 100
    and productive labour, 94
    'science' of, 162–3
    and sexuality, 97
    as skill, 59, 63, 136
    studies of, 164
    as transgression, 95–6
    in Trinidad, 113
Simmel, G., 94
Smith, A., 132–3
soap, 139
social relations, 141–2, 146–7
sociology, 120
Solomon, King, 77
specials/savers, 50–3, 61, 137
Strathern, M., 127, 165–6
    Gender of the Gift, 166
strip cartoons, 70–1
supermarkets, 11, 51, 52, 54, 167
sweets, 41, 42, 124

teenagers, 35, 103
Thatcher, M., 136
thrift, 48–62, 63, 101–4, 132–7, 161
    aesthetic of, 103–4
    aims of, 101–2
    bourgeois, 135
    British, 161
    as end, 103, 134–5, 137
    history of, 135–6
    peasant, 132–3
    in Trinidad, 136
transcendence, 19–20, 75, 78, 102, 108, 146
Trawick, M., 165

treats, 17, 40–9, 143
Trinidad, 113, 136, 165
Trobriand Islanders, 103
Tupperware, 55, 144–5
Tyler, A., 141

Valeri, V., 99, 104, 105
value line, 51
Vickery, A., 135

war memorials, 130
Weiner, A., 8, 108, 129–32, 151–2, 165–6
Weiss, B., 36–7, 38, 159
West End, 58
Wood Green, 54, 57
working class, 15, 26, 57, 135

Zimbabwe, 139